LOVE SECRETS OF THE SIGNS

ALSO BY STACEY WOLF

Secrets of the Signs
Get Psychic!

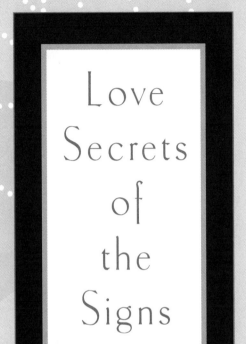

Love
Secrets
of
the
Signs

STACEY WOLF

WARNER BOOKS

An AOL Time Warner Company

Warner Books, Inc.,
1271 Avenue of the Americas, New York, NY 10020

Visit our Web site at *www.twbookmark.com*

An AOL Time Warner Company

Printed in the United States of America

First Printing: January 2002

First Trade Printing: January 2003

10 9 8 7 6 5 4 3 2 1

Library of Congress-in-Publication Data

Wolf, Stacey.
  Love secrets of the signs: astro-analyze your love life / Stacey Wolf.
    p cm.
  ISBN 0-446-67882-1
  1. Astrology. 2. Love—Miscellanea. 3. Mate selection—Miscellanea. I. Title

BF1729.L6 W65 2001
133.5'864677—dc21   2001046642

Book design and text composition by Jo Anne Metsch

To Eddie,
my novio for teaching
me about love

Contents

A sign-by-sign description of who you are and how you operate in a love relationship. The rules you need to follow for success and things you should absolutely not do for love. Plus, there's a list of the best and worst guys for you.

The best way to approach your guy, how to make the best first impression, and how to discover the key to his heart. By the time you're finished reading this, you'll know exactly how to be the girl of his dreams!

Everything you need to know to achieve balance between the signs and the sexes. All the positive and negatives of each sign combination and how to make the most of every relationship—good and bad.

Chapter Four: Dumping the Guy
117

Discover the warning signals of a relationship on its way out. Know when the party is over and it's time to make your exit. Learn sign-appropriate ways to let him down. Plus, find out how he really feels when he gets the shaft.

Chapter Five: Getting Over the Guy
131

You have high hopes at the beginning of a relationship and feel let down when it ends. Here are quick steps to get your groove back—the best things to do to find happiness, let it go, and move on to the next one!

Prelude to a Kiss: How to Use This Book

Everyone loves to be in love—whether you are looking for that perfect sweetheart, want to make the most of the guy you're with, or are pining away for your ex. Whatever stage you're at, here's all the astrological information you need to find success in love and still stay the great girl you are.

Searching for love can be really fun, but when you meet a guy, how are you supposed to know what's behind the pretty face? Yeah, you can always take a chance on him, but it's nice to know as much as possible before you dive in.

Love can be complicated. If you've been in love you know it can feel good and bad at the same time. When you first start dating it's terrific, but as time goes on obstacles appear out of nowhere. This guide shows you the best way to communicate with your sweetheart and how to make the right compromises so when you have those love woes you know what to do. We're not just talking general advice. This is totally specific to your sign, his sign, and the unique combination they make together.

When you're in a relationship, it's important that you balance your needs with that of your guy's—and it's even more important that you don't roll over like a doormat to keep him. If you have a great relationship, confirm it right here. But if you're feeling like something is just not working, don't wait it out. With *Love Secrets of the Signs,* you can spot the warning signals before they get out of hand and your self-esteem gets bulldozed.

This book takes my *Secrets of the Signs* one step further and flashes the astro-spotlight right on love and dating. If you have read that book, in addition to your Sun sign, you probably know the sign placements of the Moon, Mars, and Venus in your chart. That's great— then you can use these two books together. Here's how:

To pick the right guy in chapter 1, read your Sun, Mars, and Venus signs. The Sun is who you are, Mars tells you what type of guy you like, and Venus tells you how to act when you are in love. You may find that you are sweetly sensitive, you like guys who are guy guys, and when you are in love you are a big risk taker. The signs probably conflict a bit, but that's what makes it fun.

If you already have a guy—or at least you *like* a guy— find out his birthday. Use *Secrets of the Signs* to look up his Moon, Mars, and Venus. When you read chapter 2, "Getting the Guy," find his Sun and Venus signs. The Sun gives you his overall personality; his Venus sign tells you what type of girl he likes and how he likes to be approached.

Compare his Moon, Mars, and Venus signs to yours. Read the descriptions in chapter 3, "Keeping the Guy," for each combination to get an idea of the positives and negatives for the two of you emotionally as well as at love and play.

It's nice to know his Moon and Mars signs for chapter 4, "Dumping the Guy." When you break it off, emotions, which are ruled by the Moon, and anger, ruled by Mars, both come into play. Read the descriptions for both and take note; you'll have a more complete idea of how he'll respond to you when you do the dirty deed.

Lastly, read your Moon and Mars descriptions in chapter 5, "Getting Over the Guy." Just narrow down the explanations to your emotional well-being when reading your Moon sign, and the best activities and interests that'll help you forget him when reviewing your Mars placement.

Whether you read *Love Secrets of the Signs* on its own or whether you use it in conjunction with the other book, you will find it full of great insights and information to guide you through the love process. It'll help you find a true soul mate, avoid messy situations, and make every relationship what it is meant to be. It'll also help you find out more about yourself and how you operate in love and life. And that means more power to you!

Choosing
the
Guy

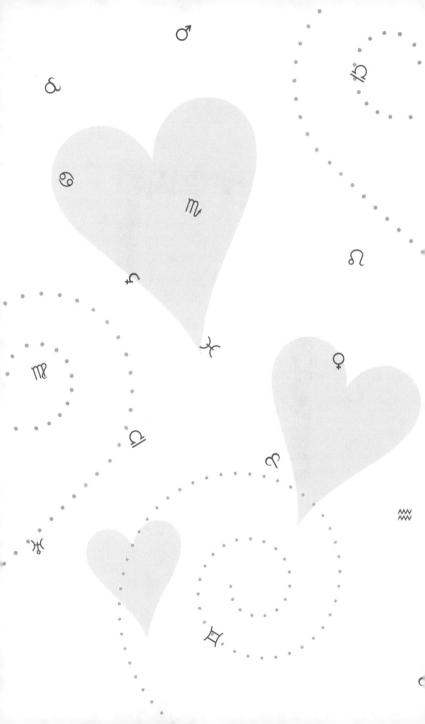

The Ram is exciting and full of energy. You always have a lot going on in your life and have little tolerance for boredom—which brings us to guys. You are impulsive in love and life. When you set your sights on a guy, you go for it with gusto. You need someone who can stand up to your Aries energy, but who's also willing to play second fiddle (at least once in a while!). Since you're so busy, the last thing you need is an insecure guy who needs a lot of reassurance.

Do's and don'ts: Do use your charm and courage to your advantage. Interested in someone? Find out what he likes and approach him. Just stop long enough to ask yourself if he likes you back. Don't waste your boundless energy on the wrong guy.

You and an Aries Guy: Best short and sweet. You may be too much alike for forever, but it'll be a wild ride while it lasts.

You and a Taurus Guy: Too stubborn for you. There can be only one leader—and you're it! He'll bound away huffing and puffing.

You and a Gemini Guy: Best sign to flirt with! There aren't two signs more suited for fun. Just watch Gemini's fickle side—you could just be hitting your stride when he disappears out the door.

You and a Cancer Guy: No wimps need apply. You'd

end up running all over this one. Aries just want to have fun—you have no time to fill his emotional needs!

You and a Leo Guy: Match made in heaven! Be loyal to your Lion and he will romance you with lavish gifts and lots of attention. Just don't try to dominate him too much or he'll let you know who rules!

You and a Virgo Guy: He's downright boring and way too critical! Skip the Virgo—the only thing he is good for is helping you with exams and papers.

You and a Libra Guy: Most popular couple. Watch for Libra's need to refine you, and don't try to throw off his delicate balance. Success in smaller doses.

You and a Scorpio Guy: Avoid him like the plague! You have too much in common—you both have explosive energy and you both like to be in charge. Better stay friends.

You and a Sagittarius Guy: Fast friends and sweethearts. You guys are on one big adventure, but you just can't slow down enough to focus on each other for long periods of time. You have a short attention span—the Sag's is shorter!

You and a Capricorn Guy: The worst possible match! Capricorns like to be very serious and sulky, while you make even the most dull task fun.

You and an Aquarius Guy: You bring out the best in each other: exploring, coming up with ways to change the world. He's all talk, you're all action—if you play along, you'll have a great time!

You and the Pisces Guy: Fun first date—then downhill quickly! A Pisces guy would love all your energy, but after a little while he'd feel chewed to pieces.

TAURUS GIRL

Romantically speaking, you are a sentimental and caring person, but might not be able to express that openly enough. You need someone who intuitively feels the comfort and safety you provide. Whoever thinks that just because you are nice you're a pushover is in for a big surprise. You also don't like to be challenged and can be obstinate at times. Avoid people who think they're automatically right.

Do's and don'ts: Do use your gentle earthy nature to get your guy's attention. Bulls have perseverance, and ultimately that can work to your advantage. Don't hold on too tight. Taureans can be possessive; too much of this is a turnoff.

You and an Aries Guy: You're friendly enough to take him in the beginning, but when your patience runs out, watch that all his energy doesn't Ram you in the butt on the way out the door.

You and a Taurus Guy: You two make loyal sweethearts. Sensitive and steadfast, once you get together, the only thing that can keep you apart is your super-stubborn nature.

You and a Gemini Guy: Forget the Gemini. He is

too shallow and chatty for the Bull. Nice to talk to at a party, but he can't have a conversation without being distracted.

You and a Cancer Guy: Sentimental squared! This sensitive, intuitive guy is perfect for you. You both love staying close to home and paying a lot of attention to each other. Wow!

You and a Leo Guy: This is bad news. Leos like to be surrounded by friends and admirers. You'd never quite know who else is after him.

You and a Virgo Guy: Made for you. He loves to spend oodles of time with you, planning the perfect dates and buying the perfect gifts. Nice.

You and a Libra Guy: Two-minute love story. Venus gives you both an appreciation of beauty, but spend time with this guy and you'll soon find out that's it.

You and a Scorpio Guy: Might be better as friends. A great match if there is stuff in your charts to soften the brooding you're both so good at.

You and a Sagittarius Guy: He's the magically disappearing man! Just when you think you've got him—poof—gone! You'll never change him; don't even try.

You and a Capricorn Guy: It's the money, honey. Here's a guy who's serious about how he spends his time. The good news is that he likes you; the bad news is that he doesn't show it.

You and an Aquarius Guy: Too unemotional for you. This guy's too busy thinking about how to improve the world to take care of you. Buh-bye.

You and a Pisces Guy: Long-lasting love! Pisces guys are so sweet and sensitive; psychic and sentimental. Grounded Taurus girls bring out the best in them.

GEMINI GIRL

Geminis are the life of the party—smart, funny, outgoing. You love to do it all, so you have a tendency to do too many things at once—and that can diffuse your energy. You need a guy who is exciting enough to keep your attention, someone who will give you the freedom to be yourself and not be jealous when you are innocently chatting with others. Turnoffs in a guy: moody, sentimental, and possessive.

Do's and don'ts: You come across as fickle because your mind and heart are often at odds. Instead of acting on impulse, try to understand both your intellect and feelings. At the first sign of trouble, don't cut your relationship short. One problem doesn't mean it's over. Take some time before closing the door.

You and an Aries Guy: Wild and crazy partner in crime. You two have so much fun together, you never stop going and going!

You and a Taurus Guy: Obstinate, slow-moving, and possessive. Are there three traits that you hate more? Doubt it. The end.

You and a Gemini Guy: Best short and sweet.

Gemini twins make great friends and sweethearts, but the huge fickleness factor would make it hard to keep this consistent.

You and a Cancer Guy: He's an emotional basket case. You like to keep things light and airy, but brooding is his middle name. When you need a good friend, call him.

You and a Leo Guy: Great date, great name-dropping. This guy is charming and popular, basically everything you want in a man. You just can't be wittier than him or he'll feel like you're stealing his thunder!

You and a Virgo Guy: He analyzes and criticizes. Virgos need to think a lot before taking action; he finds faults, too. Spontaneous Gemini can't handle it.

You and a Libra Guy: Ooh-la-la! This fellow air sign is the epitome of social grace. You couldn't ask for a more evenly matched partnership.

You and a Scorpio Guy: Run, run away, Gemini girl. This intense and secretive guy will try to own you. That's exactly what these creatures like to do.

You and a Sagittarius Guy: Best guy to flirt with. You'll have a great time, but flirting might be all you'll do. Geminis and Sags are two signs that get easily distracted.

You and a Capricorn Guy: Yuck! Traditionally serious, closed-minded, and tight-fisted. They have no fun, nothing to say, and don't want to spend all their money on you. Enough said.

You and an Aquarius Guy: Your love equal. You both

are so up on everything: the latest technologies, politics, the economy. You'll always have stuff to talk about.

You and a Pisces Guy: Mamas' boys need not apply. Here is one compassionate and sensitive guy—but face it, you hate quiet, sensitive guys!

CANCER GIRL

Cancers are emotional people, but they tend to feel things deeply and quietly. Because of that, you need a sensitive guy who can bring you out of your shell— gently. You are a complex creature. One day over- whelmed by problems, the next day you are reaching out to others who need a hand. You want a guy who under- stands and loves all the Crab's moods, good and bad—a romantic and sensitive soul who touches your heart.

Do's and don'ts: You are one of the most intuitive signs in the zodiac—do use that to avoid the wrong guys. Just make sure your insecurities don't get the best of you or you might not let yourself go when the right guy comes along. When you are hurt by something, don't automatically shut out the outside world. Tell your sweetheart how you feel.

You and an Aries Guy: Beware of fire! This ram- bunctious Ram can bulldoze all over your deep, sensi- tive feelings.

You and a Taurus Guy: Your perfect guy. He's sensitive, earthy, caring, loyal. You can get moody once in a while and it won't even matter.

You and a Gemini Guy: Chatty, chatty, chatty. This guy is all over the place. He can't sit still and he's got more nervous energy than you can handle.

You and a Cancer Guy: Too crabby for comfort. You both get very attached, but just wait until one of you feels hurt by the other—you will both shut down.

You and a Leo Guy: A great friend. Loyal, romantic, and generous with his time, he might seem like the guy of your dreams, but he's just too outgoing and independent for you.

You and a Virgo Guy: Heavenly match. This earth sign may seem a bit critical to some, but you see right through to his caring heart and soul.

The Libra Guy: Too shallow for you. Wearing the perfectly tailored outfit and mastering the art of grace and diplomacy is not on your list of priorities.

You and a Scorpio Guy: Intense. Just the way you like 'em! This guy is secretive and mysterious, but you're great at figuring out what he's feeling whether he's saying it or not.

You and a Sagittarius Guy: Unreliable and unconcerned. This guy is always off on his own adventure and can't stop his restless searching.

You and a Capricorn Guy: Hot and cold. You're both emotionally attached—only you show it and he won't. You are both loyal but you may find his detachment confusing. Worth a good try.

You and an Aquarius Guy: Don't bother, you have nothing in common, not even your habits or hobbies. He'll leave the water sign thirsty.

You and a Pisces Guy: Clingy and affectionate sweethearts. Without saying a word, you understand each other perfectly. He'll never let you out of his sight!

LEO GIRL

There is nothing a Leo loves more than romance. You ooze appeal, from the time you put on the perfect outfit and do your hair just right to when you go out on the town and hold hands with your sweetheart. Make sure you pick a guy who is also romantic, someone who'll spend time and money to show you how he appreciates you. The last thing you want is someone who takes you for granted, someone who is too busy to notice all the special things you do for love.

Do's and don'ts: Do use your flair for drama, charm, and wit to get what you want from a guy. Just make sure that once you have him, you don't try to completely dominate him. Sometimes you can seem unreasonable.

You and an Aries Guy: Love at first sight. Here's a guy who has endless energy for you. Let him feel like the star once in a while and you've got a winner.

You and a Taurus Guy: A Bull? Not in your backyard! They like to monopolize all your time and attention, and you've got way too many others around for that.

You and a Gemini Guy: Best short and sweet. Here is someone you're going to have a lot of fun with. If you try to dominate him, he'll cleverly evade capture!

You and a Cancer Guy: Make him one of your admiring fans. If you try to make it a one-on-one, you'll soon find that he is too needy and moody for you.

You and a Leo Guy: The throne belongs to you. You might last a little while with this charmer, but you both like to be adored and neither of you loves doing the adoring—see ya!

You and a Virgo Guy: A complete mismatch. He's so critical and detailed, he'll try to improve you. How dare anyone try to improve on perfection!

You and a Libra Guy: Your perfect love. Smart and sassy, this guy loves to charm and be charmed. An admirer to the max—just what you always wanted!

You and a Scorpio Guy: The worst possible match. He is quiet, secretive, jealous, emotional—ew! Besides his intense, beautiful eyes, there is nothing attractive about him.

You and a Sagittarius Guy: Love and friendship. He's on one big adventure and would love a playmate like you. Nothing you can do will bother him.

You and a Capricorn Guy: Workaholic nightmare. Capricorns have no time for titanic love and romance and could care less about being popular. Why bother?

You and an Aquarius Guy: Opposites attract. You both like being at parties—you at the center of attention, him observing in the corner. Whatever is happening here, it works for a while.

You and a Pisces Guy: The zodiac's crybaby. You have way too many people to take care of to be holding his hand and telling him everything will be all right.

VIRGO GIRL

It is hard for Virgos to relax and enjoy life. You are too busy fixing and perfecting things. You are neat and orderly and will happily help organize your friends and sweethearts. The best guy for you is one who needs a little assistance and appreciates your efforts, someone who works as hard as you do to get things done.

Do's and don'ts: When you find the right guy, do everything you can to drop your reserve and have a good time. Don't be overly critical. Your senses are so detailed that you naturally see things others don't. Bringing this stuff up isn't always the right thing to do.

You and an Aries Guy: Wild is his middle name. He'll try to get you to do all sorts of things that he considers fun; to you they seem stupid. Pass on this one.

You and a Taurus Guy: Earthly delight! Security is what you'll get if you go with this friendly Bull. You are almost too compatible—make sure to add a little spice for good measure.

You and a Gemini Guy: Better as friends. He is so spontaneous, and you like to investigate the smallest detail before you act. You'd drive each other crazy.

You and a Cancer Guy: He has needs; you like to fix things. Your emotional side will bring out his tenderness. He'll make you feel all warm and fuzzy inside!

You and a Leo Guy: Too independent to tame. He'll want attention from you but won't give back on your terms. Once in a while this would be fun.

You and a Virgo Guy: One Virgo is enough. If the two of you were planning activities and projects together, you'd get by, but once you turned your attention toward each other, you'd both get too nitpicky.

You and a Libra Guy: Lazy boy. You love his refined qualities, and he can charm you with first impressions, but you won't get him to do anything.

You and a Scorpio Guy: Love this guy! Intense, focused, driven—and he needs you. Nothing makes you happier.

You and a Sagittarius Guy: Can't fix what you can't catch. He's so happy-go-lucky that he doesn't take anything seriously. This is downright irresponsible to you.

You and a Capricorn Guy: A man after your own heart. Finally someone who sees the world exactly like you do! Together you can accomplish things you'd never do with other signs.

You and an Aquarius Guy: He's all talk, no action.

Nothing turns you off faster than a big talker. Leave him to contemplate worldly things. You've got too much to do.

You and a Pisces Guy: Help me! If anyone needs a little mending, it's this guy. He'll be flattered by your attention. Just be sure to stop at some point or he'll get his feelings hurt.

LIBRA GIRL

Libras are surrounded by an air of beauty and harmony wherever they go. This attracts many admirers—and that is one requirement in your love department: someone who gives love, attention, and a multitude of compliments. As the zodiac's partnership sign, you thrive when you are in love. The problem is that you have such high ideals built into your soul that finding the right guy can be difficult. You are likely to go through short-term relationships as you search for your perfect sweetie.

Do's and don'ts: Do explore your feelings and desires. Sometimes the scales are so busy balancing both sides of an issue that you don't know how you truly feel. Don't let outside appearances fool you. Libra's love of beauty can get in the way of finding depth in a relationship.

You and an Aries Guy: Fun for two! You love all his attention, but he's a little over-the-top sometimes. His energy can overwhelm your fine Libra balance if you're not careful.

You and a Taurus Guy: Simply down-to-earth. He's not sophisticated enough for your needs. Keep him as a friend; he likes to help people.

You and a Gemini Guy: The perfect couple. Here's a guy who's smart, funny, outgoing—basically all you need in life.

You and a Cancer Guy: Sentimental man. He loves to hang out at home with close friends, and to you this is no way to spend an evening! Keep him when you need someone to talk to.

You and a Leo Guy: Heavenly mating. This lordly Lion will romance you just the way you like it. Fine meals, nice gifts—nothing is too good for either of you.

You and a Virgo Guy: Bor-ing! The Virgo is a reserved guy, serious about his studies, and tries to improve everything he comes in contact with. You need this?

You and a Libra Guy: Social scales. You'd definitely see eye to eye, but you might end up spending too much money and time avoiding reality.

You and a Scorpio Guy: A real mental case. This guy walks around in a tornado of drama and intensity. It's too messy. You have no desire to get to know that.

You and a Sagittarius Guy: Love 'em and leave 'em. You'll have a great time, but between your indecision and his restlessness, don't expect it to last forever.

You and a Capricorn Guy: You both love money.

He likes to keep it; you like to spend it. Put the Goat out to pasture.

You and an Aquarius Guy: Two peas in a pod—almost! You have a lot in common with this Aquarius; you'll just be surprised every once in a while when his stubbornness comes out.

You and a Pisces Guy: Way too sensitive. Weepy Pisces guys are best left alone. They'll find someone to comfort them—it just shouldn't be you!

SCORPIO GIRL

Scorpios are intensely creative and passionate about everything they do. Even the simplest task is completed with some help from mysterious forces. With you, it's all or nothing. You like to totally get to know your sweethearts, to possess them. You are direct and loyal, attracting only the deepest and most satisfying love. Some may cower at this intensity, but your perfect mate will revel in all that love, honesty, and commitment. Avoid people who are wrapped up in thinking instead of feeling.

Do's and Don'ts: Do use that air of mystery to your advantage. You can make a guy like you without saying a word. Don't let your jealousy and resentment get the best of you. Ask yourself if something is going on or are you just seeing it that way.

You and an Aries Guy: Rubs you the wrong way. This guy is way too pushy and self-interested. Get out of his way or make him get out of yours.

You and a Taurus Guy: Clash of the Titans. Two big personalities, and both can be stubborn and moody. If you can get past that, you'll find a pretty good match.

You and a Gemini Guy: He is too flirty and flighty. You want to help heal the world, and this guy only wants to talk about himself. Get real.

You and a Cancer Guy: A guy after your own heart. Compassionate, intuitive, clingy—just what you always wanted in a guy.

You and a Leo Guy: A big turnoff! Outgoing, showy, dramatic—who does this guy think he is?

You and a Virgo Guy: A definite keeper. Every Scorpio needs a reserved, caring, well-organized Virgo hanging around and picking up after them.

You and a Libra Guy: Too balance-obsessed for you. And believe me, you like to be obsessed, just not with harmony and equality. Live a little!

You and a Scorpio Guy: And you think *you're* suspicious!? You love his creativity and intensity, but you'd quickly complain that he is secretive, jealous, and brooding. Sound familiar?

You and a Sagittarius Guy: No follow-through. At first you love his adventurous nature until you quickly realize that he doesn't go any deeper than the surface.

You and a Capricorn Guy: Conservative and economical. You like to keep track of your own life, and this guy is always telling you how to do things right. Yuck.

You and an Aquarius Guy: Best short and sweet. You have a lot in common and you both love to make the world a better place, but that's where it ends. Buh-bye!

You and a Pisces Guy: The way to go! A Pisces guy thinks you are absolutely terrific, no matter what you do. He'll read your mind and excuse your moods, too.

SAGITTARIUS GIRL

Sags are the adventurers of the universe. You are so cheerful that it appears you don't have a care in the world. As a friend you're always reaching out a hand, and you never expect anything in return. The downside: Your restless nature makes it hard for you to settle down. You need a guy who will give you freedom and excitement. And he must have an unconventional outlook on life. Clingy, insecure, and jealous types are the worst for you.

Do's and don'ts: You have such a universal way of looking at romance; do bring that down to a smaller scope to keep a relationship. Don't avoid drama and emotions at all costs. You can strike a balance between your needs and those of your sweetie.

You and an Aries Guy: He's a great match for you. He's fun, friendly, adventurous, and he'll accept you as you are. Just tell him how wonderful he is every once in a while.

You and a Taurus Guy: Too loyal for your taste. He wants to protect you and provide for you—and that's the last thing you want! You like doing things for yourself.

You and a Gemini Guy: Fun and flirty! This is a great relationship—just don't expect it to last. You both have short attention spans when it comes to members of the opposite sex.

You and a Cancer Guy: They don't play. Don't be surprised if you never run into this guy; he's always at home discussing his feelings with friends. Two things you never do!

You and a Leo Guy: Keep this one! You're not much for commitment, and the Lion will give you freedom and adventure. All you have to do in return is give him your adoration.

You and a Virgo Guy: Keep away. He'll just try to pin you down and change your wild ways. Dump him!

You and a Scorpio Guy: Best short and sweet. At first you'd hit it off big, but you'd soon find him way too intense for your fly-by-night nature.

You and a Sagittarius Guy: Love 'em and leave 'em and love 'em again! Two Sags think the grass is greener over there, but they always come home, too.

You and a Capricorn Guy: All work and no play. There's no good reason to be hanging out with this one. Really.

You and an Aquarius Guy: Perfect love! A guy who

loves an open-minded, adventurous, playful girl like you. He won't ask too much of you, either.

You and a Pisces Guy: Way too wimpy. He'll enjoy talking to you because you'll cheer him up, but he'll go on and on . . .

CAPRICORN GIRL

Although Capricorns show the world their quiet and serious side, you have a lot of other things going on that only the most patient and loving friends, family, and sweethearts ever discover. You are loving, loyal, protective, and have a sense of humor, too. You need a guy who'll take the time to nurture those special qualities. You attract either of two types: someone who likes to set goals and accomplish things, or someone who is a little lost and needs loving and protecting.

Do's and don'ts: Do stop focusing on your ambitions long enough to see what's out there. There's a lot of fun to be had, but Capricorns have to go out of their way to find it. Don't hold on to past hurts. If someone did something to hurt you, chances are it wasn't intentional.

You and an Aries Guy: His mantra: Follow me! Follow me! After a bit of this you'd go crazy. You've got better things to do than let him drag you around.

You and a Taurus Guy: Love is serious business. When it comes to work and love, you're both on the same page. He's a keeper.

You and a Gemini Guy: Fun to flirt with but not to go out with. He's all over the place and spreads himself too thin. You need more time than he's willing to give.

You and a Cancer Guy: This sensitive guy will melt your heart. He'll bring out your feminine side and read your mind, too.

You and a Leo Guy: Drama king. Here's something you can live without: a larger-than-life, flirtatious, dominating charmer.

You and a Virgo Guy: Efficient energy. When a Capricorn and a Virgo get together, they love to work for love. This kind of energy will make for some interesting dates.

You and a Libra Guy: Blah, blah, blah. You can't participate in idle chatter; it goes against the core of your being. Will he want to discuss real things? No.

You and a Scorpio Guy: He's way out. If you're in the mood for adventure, he's the best of the bunch. You'll get smothered by him and love it.

You and a Sagittarius Guy: Spend one night with a Sag and you'll never want to do it again. He's too carefree and reckless for your serious sensibilities.

You and a Capricorn Guy: Fifty-fifty. You'll certainly see the world through the same window—which is important for you—but you might have a hard time sharing your deepest secrets and feelings with each other.

You and an Aquarius Guy: Too much. All this guy talks about is making the world a better place. You're busy managing your own life, thank you.

You and a Pisces Guy: Positively dreamy. This romantic, sweet, and sensitive guy knows how to give you exactly the kind of love and attention you can't put into words.

AQUARIUS GIRL

Outgoing and independent, Aquarians are great friends and sweethearts. Your universal frame of mind keeps you somewhat detached, and your sweetie will have to be comfortable with that. You need a guy who will be able to talk technology and politics, someone who has the same unconventional attitudes and is curious about life. You don't need a moody, overemotional guy whose sentimental attachments keep him from learning and growing.

Do's and don'ts: Making the world a better place is great, but do make sure you're also there for your love, one-on-one, as well. Don't allow yourself to get jealous at the drop of a hat. Aquarians misunderstand people's motivations sometimes and think the worst.

You and an Aries Guy: An attentive sweetheart. He has a lot of energy to direct your way, and you love it. Your relationship will be very spontaneous and fiery.

You and a Taurus Guy: Too homey. You like your guys smart, sophisticated, and worldly. His mind is on more down-to-earth things. You'll never see eye to eye.

You and a Gemini Guy: Your airy partner in crime.

Here's a guy made from the same mold. He's funny, fast, spontaneous, open-minded—what's not to like?

You and a Cancer Guy: Mushy and overemotional. Just what you need, someone who can't control his feelings. Don't go there.

You and a Leo Guy: A special love. This guy'll do whatever it takes to win you over, and you'll love every minute of it. You just might get annoyed that he's always on stage.

You and a Virgo Guy: Your worst nightmare— someone who'll take one look at you and tell you what needs fixing. You'll have no problem telling him what's on your mind, either.

You and a Libra Guy: The perfect party of two. No matter if you're planning to stay home and watch a movie, this guy'll make it a special event.

You and a Scorpio Guy: Secretive, suspicious, brooding, energetic—a taste of this guy's everyday mood swings. You'll say you don't need it.

You and a Sagittarius Guy: The wanderers. This is the most adventuresome pair in the zodiac. You'll have more fun than you ever thought possible. Go for it.

You and a Capricorn Guy: Romancing the stone. He's closed-minded, serious, and emotionally cold. Everything that you dislike in a guy.

You and an Aquarius Guy: Bring out the best and worst in each other. You'll agree on most things, but two of you together might get stubborn and remote, so watch out.

You and a Pisces Guy: Better as friends. You both

have very intuitive ways of looking at the world, but he's too bleeding-heart for you.

PISCES GIRL

Pisces is one of the most sensitive, romantic, and dreamy signs. Once you feel safe in a relationship, you dote on your guy with constant affection. The downside: When you feel ignored, you can act out quite impulsively. You also live in your own little world. You need a guy who wants to protect you, provide you with stability, and who will enjoy hanging out in that reality of yours.

Do's and don'ts: Do use your intuition and femininity to capture that special someone, but don't let him trample all over you just to keep him. Don't pretend your famous emotional supersensitivity doesn't exist. Avoiding what is bothering you will only make things worse.

You and an Aries Guy: Your worst nightmare. You'll appreciate his strong will at first, but after he runs you over with it, you'll throw in the towel.

You and a Taurus Guy: Here's a guy you can cling to and he'll love it. Adoring him is easy when he wants to take care of your every need.

You and a Gemini Guy: Leave him at the party. You'll have a fun exchange of ideas, but he's unfocused and emotionally unavailable.

You and a Cancer Guy: Perrrrfect! You have such an innate understanding of each other, you'll feel like you've known him forever.

You and a Leo Guy: Luxury and romance—at first. Yes, you'll adore him, but his need to be the boss can make it tough to continue.

You and a Virgo Guy: A loyal sweetheart. He'll be very attentive and help you with anything you need, but watch out—he'll criticize you till the cows come home.

You and a Libra Guy: Good for a date. You have enough in common to talk at a party, but he's too unemotional and oddly balanced for your taste.

You and a Scorpio Guy: Long-lasting love. This compassionate and intuitive guy'll want to completely own you—and you'll love letting him.

You and a Sagittarius Guy: Here today, gone tomorrow. This is a guy who looks charming and attentive, but comes and goes depending on the weather.

You and a Capricorn Guy: Quietly sensitive. He's cold on the outside, warm on the inside—and you see right through him. This one is a keeper.

You and an Aquarius Guy: Keep him as a friend. You both have a lot in common—he'd reach out a hand to anyone in need, and so would you. He's just a bit impersonal for your nature.

You and a Pisces Guy: The good: You'll feel complete with another intuitive Fish. The bad: Your procrastination is quadrupled, and so is the whine. You love it, but not forever.

Getting

the

Guy

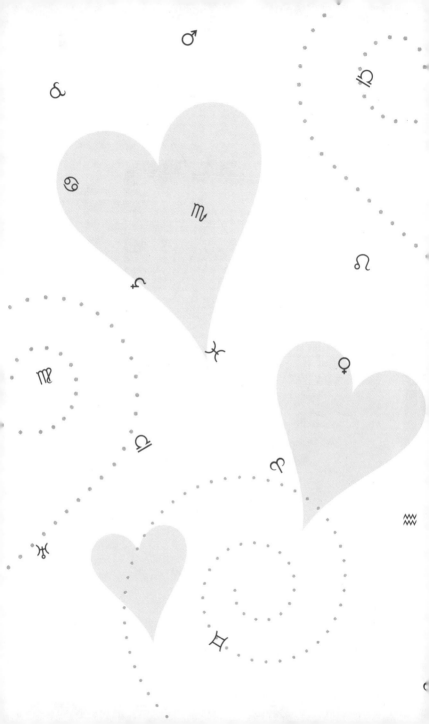

CAPTURING AN ARIES

Aries guys are independent thinkers; they love to hatch schemes and live dangerously. They are always on the move and get bored really easily. In love they are very affectionate and idealistic. He's always fun to be around, but can be argumentative—sometimes for no good reason. He needs a girl who can be a pal as well as a sweetheart, someone who'll stick by him and not take it personally when he's in the mood to stir things up a bit.

Best way to approach him: Let him know you like him, but then wait for him to make the big moves. This may not be easy. You can't be too subtle with him, because he just doesn't see those small details. On the other hand, he likes to be the one doing the chasing. You can play a little hard-to-get with this guy. He likes a challenge, but he also likes success. If he doesn't see immediate results, he'll lose interest.

Fast track to his heart: With your sweetest and sassiest voice, ask him to take you out for a big adventure—a night out on the town or a wild afternoon of whitewater rafting. Tell him you want it to be a surprise, that whatever he wants will be really fun.

How to be the girl of his dreams: He likes to be a macho man, so let him think he's leading! Tell him how great he is, ask for his help, then sing his praises—a lot. He is very proud of himself and loves attention, and that'll give him yet another opportunity to shine. Be his playmate and always be fun. Use your creativity to constantly keep things exciting. If he's bored, he may move on.

CAPTURING A TAURUS

The Taurus guy is determined and dependable on the outside, sweet and sentimental on the inside. He is easygoing but likes to get his own way. The Bull loves his friends and family and is constantly doing favors for everyone he knows. He enjoys working and accomplishing things, going at his own pace but never giving up. Taurus guys need a girl who is assertive and independent but intuitive enough not to push, someone who needs a little taking care of but likes to do some pampering in return.

Best way to approach him: You'll definitely have to do the approaching. Tauruses are on the shy side, but don't worry about saying the right thing. Give him a sweet look or a light touch on the arm—not too much or it'll turn him off. Tauruses are practical guys and like to collect things, so he must have some things at home that he is sentimentally attached to. Find out what they are and you're golden!

Fast track to his heart: Bake him cookies (make sure they're good!). Give them to him and tell him what a nice guy he is—he loves food and he likes being appreciated, too.

How to be the girl of his dreams: The Bull is traditional and loves down-to-earth girls, so don't be too assertive, and don't wear gobs of makeup or tight clothes. Au naturel and a nice pair of jeans is perfect for him. It's easy to be his sweetheart, since he is a loyal guy who likes simple pleasures. He loves to stay close to home and cuddle. He also likes a home-cooked meal. Every once in a while, give him a cute keepsake. Something nice but practical that reminds him of you.

CAPTURING A GEMINI

Social Gemini guy is constantly on the go. He has friends around every corner and too many hobbies to keep up with. He is a quick thinker and always has a joke on the tip of his tongue. He likes to hang out with a lot of people and innocently flirt with everyone. Gemini guys need a girl made from the same mold—smart, funny, into experiencing new things, and, most of all, friendly. But because he's got a million interests, he might not have much time for deep romantic and emotional attachments.

Best way to approach him: Talk to him about everything. First read up on the latest trends in politics and pop culture, and then talk to him. He loves people in the know. Put his e-mail address on your buddy list and look for him after hours. He spends a lot of time talking on the computer and the phone, too.

Fast track to his heart: Find out where the next cool party is going to be (or create one) and invite him before he hears about it from someone else. He'll be very impressed that you have friends in high places, and he always loves a party.

How to be the girl of his dreams: Be curious about life. He likes people with a casual, adventurous attitude. Be his best friend, not a mushy, clingy girlfriend. Being bored is his worst nightmare, so he'll never slow down. The key to sticking around: Keep up with him and always go with the flow. Don't be too possessive or overemotional; he's too busy to be tied down and will want out pretty fast if he doesn't have his freedom.

CAPTURING A CANCER

The Cancer guy, a Moon child, is always ruled by his deep unconscious emotions and feelings. That is the reason he can be so approachable one day and withdrawn the next. He is sentimental about everything, likes to keep in touch with old friends, and keeps many mementos from the past. Cancers love to be in relationships, but take their time falling in love. A fear of getting hurt weighs heavily on his mind, but once he starts to open up he gets very attached and never lets go.

Best way to approach him: Find him in a good mood, then tell him about your problems, feelings, and insecurities. Make him feel safe and secure and he'll start to let his own feelings out. If you notice that he is in a bad mood, give him silent comfort and space. Most likely he'll want to work out his problems on his own.

Fast track to his heart: Invite him for a picnic in the park. He enjoys nature and quiet afternoons with friends, so it's a big plus to find a gal pal who likes him enough to prepare lunch, too!

How to be the girl of his dreams: Cancers love a homebody. Give him a taste of the traditional side of you. Nurture him and make him feel loved and secure. Because he is sensitive and reserved, a Cancer's girlfriend has to be able to understand his moods and intuitively know what he needs, since he will rarely tell you. If you want to get a Cancer to fall in love with you, be aware that he doesn't take love lightly. The quality he appreciates most is loyalty. Once he's in love, he'll stick with you through thick and thin, and will expect the same. If you can't do that, skip him.

CAPTURING A LEO

Leos have a lot of energy. They love life and love to be center stage. They have a high view of themselves and their accomplishments and love to rule like royalty. Since the Lion likes to make sure he is constantly surrounded by admirers, he is very generous with his time, attention, and especially his money. There has never been a Leo yet that doesn't have a big wallet when it comes to gifts for himself or others. Watch out for a Leo who has had a bad day—he can get lazy and arrogant, expecting everyone to bow to his wishes. Thankfully, this doesn't last for too long.

Best way to approach him: Tell him how fabulous he is, get him to talk about himself, and just listen as if what he is saying is the most interesting stuff you have ever heard in your life! Don't disagree with him unless you do it subtly. He'll think you are wonderful in no time.

Fast track to his heart: Put on a sensational dress and heels, do your hair and makeup to the max (they love flamboyant and feminine), and go with him to the finest restaurant in town. Let him show you off. Tell him that nothing is too good for him!

How to be the girl of his dreams: Let him be a manly man! Let him plan the dates, pay the bill, and talk all he wants while you're together. Leos like to dominate. You can get your way with your Lion guy by using flattery. He is a sucker for a compliment. Say it right and you can get him to do anything (say it wrong and you're in for a huge argument!). He loves luxury, too. Give him a piece of jewelry or a nice shirt for no reason other than that he is so special!

CAPTURING A VIRGO

Virgo guys have a sensible and practical nature. Detail-oriented big time, these guys have X-ray vision when it comes to accomplishing important projects. He enjoys being in relationships, but might not look for them as much as some other signs do. Once he's hooked, he will constantly be looking for little things that he can do for you. Just watch that his attention to detail isn't focused in your direction for too long. Virgos have a tendency to get hypercritical, and he might want to make you one of his famous fix-it projects. That's not good for your ego.

Best way to approach him: Quietly! Find out how he spends his time, then talk to him about that. Ask him for help reorganizing the files on your computer or to go shopping for new software with you. Let him do stuff for you; it'll make him feel needed.

Fast track to his heart: Take him to a car show (or anyplace he can examine facts and figures!), where he can look at all the new models and study their designs. Let him tell you all about the practical car he'd like to get one day and all the things it can do.

How to be the girl of his dreams: This guy is sweet but doesn't like to show his feelings. He'd much rather analyze things. He likes a girl who is reserved, kind, and organized. Always have your hair done and a nice outfit on—no ripped jeans. He needs to feel secure in your relationship, so always make sure he knows how much you appreciate all he does for you. Do little special things for him without him asking. He'll notice the small details and feel comforted by your efforts.

CAPTURING A LIBRA

Social and charming, Libra can talk to anybody about anything. But that doesn't mean he likes them, because in addition to being charming, he is also a good actor. Libras love to be in relationships and continually search for their perfect partner. The problem is that if they don't find perfection, they lose interest and move on. The bad side of the Scales: He can get a bit lazy and self-centered sometimes.

Best way to approach him: Libras have a great sense of style and class. Ask him to help you pick out new decorations for your room or clothing for a special date (with him?).

Fast track to his heart: He loves luxury and art. Take him to the most elegant restaurant you can afford and top it off with a show or a concert. Compliment him on his clothes—no doubt they are chosen perfectly for the occasion. Talk to him about politics, fashion trends, and him, of course.

How to be the girl of his dreams: He strives for balance and harmony in life, so whatever you do, don't upset the apple cart! Take everything in stride. If you want to disagree with him, you may find yourself losing the debate because Libras like to play devil's advocate. Just don't lose your temper or he'll automatically shut off. Libras like women who are beautiful and have understated grace in their clothes and mannerisms.

Don't be too loud, dress too wild, or act like a prima donna or he won't want to be seen with you.

CAPTURING A SCORPIO

The first thing people notice about a Scorpio guy is his driving intensity. Independent, creative, and deeply emotional, he is passionate about everything he does or he wouldn't bother doing it in the first place. He inspires others to do the same. Scorpio guys don't give their hearts away easily, but once they do, they will demand your full attention. In return, they are loyal, honest, and very sincere. But watch out—at the drop of a hat he can get jealous and resentful for no apparent reason at all.

Best way to approach him: Talk to him about meaningful things; the state of the world and the environment are good topics. Be as opinionated as you can (but a tad less so than him). Just make sure you know what you're talking about and you don't say something because you think he wants to hear it or he'll get turned off.

Fast track to his heart: Do something cool that takes no money at all. He'll be impressed that you are into deeper things than money can buy. Take him to your secret hideouts. Share with him your deepest fears and psychic experiences.

How to be the girl of his dreams: Be romantic. Read his mind. Totally let him into your life. Scorpios live on feelings and intuition and like to really get to know their sweethearts. Be interesting outside of knowing him. Volunteer somewhere, read books about past lives, and write letters to your congressman or -woman. Just don't spend too much time away from him or he'll think the worst; then it'll be up to you to prove otherwise.

CAPTURING A SAGITTARIUS

Outgoing and fun, Sagittarius thinks every day is a new adventure. You'll find that he is constantly in a restless search for new experiences, something to teach him about the meaning of life. Always willing to lend a hand, never needing anything in return, he is the most friendly sign of the zodiac. What you see is what you get. He says what he means in a direct but not always tactful way. As a boyfriend, he is never jealous but sometimes comes across as indifferent when his mind is focused on other things. It's very hard to get this guy to commit for a long time. To him, his need for freedom outweighs the benefits of love.

Best way to approach him: Be a feminine pal, a best friend as well as a sweetie. Talk to him about where he wants to travel. Ask him about his favorite adventure. Be light and fun and full of interesting experiences of your own. Laugh at his stories; be sincere.

Fast track to his heart: Invite him on a hike or a bike

ride to a place neither of you has been before. Go to a carnival, ride the rides and sample all the food. Don't be afraid of trying new things while you are there.

How to be the girl of his dreams: Be easygoing and give him lots of freedom. Let him know that whatever he wants to do is fine with you. This guy runs away when he feels that he's being roped into something, so don't be clingy, needy, or deeply emotional around him. Make every day exciting to keep him around, because unfortunately he has a short attention span. If he's off on his own escapade, find another guy to flirt with. You might not make him jealous, but he'll want you more when someone else wants you, too.

CAPTURING A CAPRICORN

Under that Capricorn reserve is a loyal, earthy, and affectionate guy. The problem is that he just can't show it. The Goat is great at concealing his feelings and emotions, and is completely self-contained and self-sufficient. He enjoys working and tackling projects from the bottom up. Getting to the top takes time, and he is willing to put in the work and wait for it. Capricorns play just as hard, taking their hobbies seriously, too. Because of that, they find success in everything they do.

Best way to approach him: Let him know that you notice and appreciate all his hard work. Talk to him about his goals and ambitions, his life plan. Tell him about yours, just make sure they are well thought out. Nothing turns him off more than a flighty person.

Fast track to his heart: Find out what he takes seriously, what he studies and wishes to accomplish, then let him know you are just as interested in those things as he is. Find out if there is a lecture about one of his favorite topics and ask him to go with you.

How to be the girl of his dreams: The girlfriend of a Capricorn has to appreciate all the work he does to create a secure future and see past his layers of restraint. You can lighten him up a bit, but don't be flamboyant and aggressive. He likes to see the same reserve, work skills, and study habits in his friends and sweethearts. There is just so much time in a day and he is very specific about the people whom he chooses to spend it with. He has a hard time with emotions—the only thing you'll see is resentment building and steam coming out of his ears. You may have to use your female intuition to find out what is really going on there.

CAPTURING AN AQUARIUS

Offbeat and unusual is the Aquarian nature. He strives to be unconventional and really dislikes closed-minded people. Your independent Aquarian is a seeker of knowledge and adventure. Lost in the depths of his mind, he can come across as detached when it comes to his love life. If you can deal with that, he can be an attentive sweetheart. Because he is always off somewhere exploring the universe, his emotions can sneak up on him when he least expects it, going from laid-back to defiant and jealous in a matter of seconds.

Best way to approach him: Hand him a complicated electronic gadget and ask him to help you figure out how to use it. While you're at it, discuss his favorite ways to improve the world.

Fast track to his heart: Do something different. Get a group of creative, open-minded thinkers together for a poetry reading. Go out for coffee and discuss classic sixties literature or ultramodern philosophy. Have an insightful opinion.

How to be the girl of his dreams: Be friendly, creative, and well-read. He likes an intellectual girl, someone who can discuss humanitarian issues and the latest technology and knows what she is talking about. Don't be too demanding on his time and emotions. He might not run away, but he definitely can't stand up to that kind of challenge. Do things with his friends, because he likes hanging out in groups. Don't take it personally if he needs some time alone—that's just his way.

CAPTURING A PISCES

Sensitive and understanding, Pisces guys have a way of getting into your soul. They are the ultra-romantics of the zodiac and live in their dreams. Very idealistic in love, they want to create the love of their lives, a princess for their knight in shining armor. Since the Pisces guy is a bit insecure and indecisive, he may need a push in the right direction. He also doesn't like to see the bright lights of reality, and this can lead him to not accepting things as they really are. This will never change. Either journey into his special world, create your own together, or don't even bother.

Best way to approach him: No doubt he is a writer or musician. Ask him to play you a song or read you something he has written. Encourage him, tell him how creative and artistic he is. Ask him about his spiritual beliefs, and share yours with him.

Fast track to his heart: Compose him a love poem and give it to him with a rose. Hide a box of chocolates in his locker with a note. Whisper sweet nothings on his voice mail.

How to be the girl of his dreams: Be compassionate, not only to him, but to strangers and animals as well—that'll score you some big points. Don't be too critical or judgmental or he'll just shut down real fast. Dote on him just like he will dote on you, and cling as much as you want. Here's a guy who loves to get to the bottom of your emotional well. Don't take advantage of his goodwill—he'll do whatever he can to please you and can't say no. Give him lots of hugs and reminders of how you feel about him.

Keeping

the

Guy

ARIES GIRL

Aries Girl and Aries Guy

On the plus side: You have the same energy and love of life. You're never bored with each other.

The negatives: Two leaders, one relationship—it just doesn't add up. This can be the cause of some explosive exchanges.

Finding the balance: Make sure you each do a lot of interesting things outside of the relationship. That way you'll be more content to share the limelight while you are together. Practice giving each other the right of way. Think before you speak and take time to cool off before you say something you're going to regret.

Aries Girl and Taurus Guy

On the plus side: Short-term, you can inspire the Taurus guy to take more risks and have some fun. He can teach you patience.

The negatives: When you try to get your way, he just gets more stubborn. The more obstinate he gets, the more you push. The end.

Finding the balance: This is a tough combination to make long-term. You can slow down your pace to better match his and try not to make him do what you want so often. Get him to go on your adventures more or let you go alone without feeling like he comes second. Make your escapades closer to home and he won't feel so uncomfortable.

Aries Girl and Gemini Guy

On the plus side: You both like constant adventures, hate to be bored, and are very chatty.

The negatives: You both like to start things and not finish them. Gemini guy likes his freedom and might not always be available when you want him. You can both find other people to divert your attention.

Making the most of it: Make sure you give your Gemini enough space and don't take him for granted. Make an extra effort to communicate when you get busy with your own stuff. Don't let him see your temper too often.

Aries Girl and Cancer Guy

On the plus side: He likes to hang around, so you'll always have someone to play with. He can use some of your infectious energy!

The negatives: When you are both in a bad mood, neither of you is going to bend to the other. You can get sick of his crabby, clingy ways; he can get offended by your in-your-face style.

Making the most of it: You'll have to be less demanding and more intuitive. He'll have to be willing to stop whining and actually leave the house once in a while.

Aries Girl and Leo Guy

On the plus side: You are two peas in a pod, dynamic, outgoing, adventurous.

The negatives: You both are headstrong and big on the melodramatic emotional responses. You may have some overblown arguments.

Making the most of it: Even you can't beat the Leo. Let him lead; he'll give you enough power to command his army, and you'll still get your control fix in when you need it. Disagreements are bound to happen, so don't take them personally.

Aries Girl and Virgo Guy

On the plus side: You like to start things and he likes to finish them. You like to lead, he likes to use his energy in service to others.

The negatives: You think you are fabulous, while he is going to find lots of things about you to pick at. There is nothing you hate more than a nag!

Making the most of it: This is tough. You can try to be less impulsive (but it's not going to work for long!). Help that Virgo to be more spontaneous and less reserved. Be as gentle as you can and take his criticisms lightly. Whatever you do, don't open up and let him have it.

Aries Girl and Libra Guy

On the plus side: You are both pleasure seekers. You like to be flattered, and he is good at charming people.

The negatives: Sometimes you can be too brash for his fine social senses. Your energy can shake up his balanced scales.

Making the most of it: Be very intuitive about his natural need for balance. When he's had enough, don't try to force him into things. Relax—you don't always need to be on the go. Don't pick fights with him. Libras really dislike emotional outbursts.

Aries Girl and Scorpio Guy

On the plus side: Honestly, the only thing in common here is that you are both breathing.

The negatives: Your independence brings out Scorpio's jealous streak. He'll always think you are hiding something and doing something behind his back, and that'll drive you nuts. Lots of arguments.

Making the most of it: Since you both have a lot of energy and like to do things that are important to you, make sure you stay busy. If you are tired when you get together, chances are you can avoid some of the mess.

Aries Girl and Sagittarius Guy

On the plus side: You are both free spirits. You love to explore and are constantly moving on to bigger and better things.

The negatives: The weakness is that there isn't a whole lot of staying power. You're also both really direct and can say things impulsively.

Making the most of it: This should be easy for both of you. If you have a misunderstanding, try to talk about it calmly. Also, tone down the blunt comments—once something is said, you can't take it back.

Aries Girl and Capricorn Guy

On the plus side: Aries have a lot of short bursts of energy and Capricorns have it long-term. If you like each other, at least you'll never give up.

The negatives: You like to spend, he likes to save, and you both like to take the lead. He'll have judgments against your lifestyle, and you'll get pissed at that.

Making the most of it: Coax him out of his closed-minded habits, take him on an adventure and share the control. Don't try to boss him around, and listen to him once in a while or he'll get resentful.

Aries Girl and Aquarius Guy

On the plus side: You're both full of energy and are always up for doing new things. You're both opinion-ated so your conversations are feisty.

The negatives: Aquarian guy may be a bit too aloof for you and is not going to follow you around at your whim, so get used to it.

Making the most of it: Tell him if you're not getting

what you need and he'll bend over backwards to give it to you. Give him his freedom; he needs a bit more than you do. Know that he might not always agree with you, but to him that's part of the fun.

Aries Girl and Pisces Guy

On the plus side: Pisces guys can get addicted to all your bubbly energy. They love being in love and will adore your every move.

The negatives: The same energy that he adores can be this relationship's undoing. The fantasy of who he thinks you are will crash into reality and he will not be able to handle it. Ouch.

Making the most of it: Cultivate your sensitive, intuitive side and use it to figure out what's going on in his head. Be subtle with your thoughts and feelings. Don't get frustrated with his wishy-washy ways.

TAURUS GIRL

Taurus Girl and Aries Guy

On the plus side: You're both affectionate. The Bull can help settle the impulsive energy of the Ram—as long as he will let you.

The negatives: He likes to do things impulsively and you like to stick to routine. You feel smothered by his forceful energy.

Making the most of it: This might be worth a short run, but it's difficult. Aries are good at coming up with ideas and you are good at following them through, so find common interests and you have a shot at getting along. Don't get frustrated at his aggressiveness or it's over.

Taurus Girl and Taurus Guy

On the plus side: You are both security-conscious and hardworking. Once you're in love, you both want it to last.

The negatives: You're both stubborn and like to get your way. The union could get a little boring if both of you stick by your normal routine.

Making the most of it: Make a big effort to plan fun things to do together. Go out separately with different friends from the zodiac. Taureans can get involved in work too easily and skip the romance, so you have to make sure that doesn't happen.

Taurus Girl and Gemini Guy

On the plus side: Geminis like people and Taureans make great friends. He'll get through your reserve and make you laugh.

The negatives: You are very set in your ways, while the Gemini guy is a very changeable character. He doesn't like your slow pace. You don't like his fidgety restlessness.

Making the most of it: You can help focus the Gemini energy in a practical and creative way. He can inspire you and liven you up. But after the initial interest is over, you may not have enough to keep this going. You like a deeper commitment than he'll ever give you.

Taurus Girl and Cancer Guy

On the plus side: Both of you are sentimental homebodies. He likes to cling and you like being possessive. It's really perfect.

The negatives: You can both get moody without ever telling the other what is bothering you. In fact, you're both stubborn in this way, but against a Cancer you win, hands down.

Making the most of it: Plan cozy evenings together, do things close to home where you can have quiet fun and hold hands a lot. Offer to do things for him when he feels down. Show him you love him without saying a word. Easy enough!

Taurus Girl and Leo Guy

On the plus side: You are both loyal and full of pride. As long as that isn't hurt you've got a chance.

The negatives: Where to begin? The Leo likes to be worshipped and you have no tolerance for his dramatic displays. He thinks you are stubborn beyond help.

Making the most of it: In the beginning you may

have some luck, because every Leo likes a kingdom. He'll be very attentive and generous in order to woo you into his world. You like the attention but can't be led anywhere. When he figures this out, he's going to get mad; then you are going to get even more stubborn.

Taurus Girl and Virgo Guy

On the plus side: You both crave security and will naturally give that to each other. You both enjoy working hard and accomplishing things.

The negatives: When the Virgo gets nitpicky, you quickly get sulky. You don't like anyone criticizing you and telling you what to do.

Making the most of it: Plan your dates and projects together. Praise each other often. You both love when your efforts are noticed. Since neither of you likes life on the wild side, go out of your way to be more spontaneous and fun.

Taurus Girl and Libra Guy

On the plus side: Libra guys are very charming and romantic, and you love all the attention. You are good at stabilizing his wobbly balance.

The negatives: You dislike his loose spending habits. He has a much more lighthearted approach to love than you do.

Making the most of it: You do have enough in common to make this work for a short time, but don't expect too much. Give your Libra the room he needs and don't try to hold on to him. Do little things for him without getting annoyed. Buy each other gifts: Tauruses like collectibles; Libras have more highbrow tastes.

Taurus Girl and Scorpio Guy

On the plus side: You share a lot of passion and commitment for things you choose to do. You're both very ambitious.

The negatives: Your two big personalities can get jealous and possessive. There's definitely a lot of head-butting here.

Making the most of it: Find activities and projects you can both pour your energies into. If there is a misunderstanding, don't automatically dig in your heels for a tug-of-war. Neither one of you will be able to control the other, so you'll have to find a middle ground that feels comfortable to both of you.

Taurus Girl and Sagittarius Guy

On the plus side: The Sag guy accepts you exactly as you are, and that makes you feel safe (but only when you are with him!). You like his easygoing nature.

The negatives: The risky attitude of Sagittarians scares the cautious Bull. Taureans get frustrated by the Archer's constant wanderings and lack of commitment.

Making the most of it: This won't be easy for long—you'll have to let go of the idea of possessing him. He needs 100 percent freedom to come and go as he pleases without hearing an earful. In return, he'll need to downplay his casual ways and take everything a bit more seriously.

Taurus Girl and Capricorn Guy

On the plus side: You have the same nature. You both want security and you're willing to work for it. You're both loyal and do a lot for your sweethearts.

The negatives: There's not much in the way of excitement and fun. Neither one of you finds it easy to talk openly about your feelings.

Making the most of it: You both need lots of hugs and gentle reassurance. Make sure that if you have a problem saying it, you show it instead. Both Capricorns and Taureans like to do things their own way; in this case compromise is the best idea.

Taurus Girl and Aquarius Guy

On the plus side: It's a bit of a stretch, but both the Bull and the Waterbearer make great friends—though not necessarily with each other.

The negatives: The Aquarian is always a bit detached. He lives in his mind, and the Taurus just can't go there. You'll get frustrated at not being able to hold on.

Making the most of it: Channel your energies into completing one of your Aquarian's humanitarian schemes (that is, if the conservative Taurus doesn't think it's too crazy). Give him the freedom to come and go as he pleases. Appeal to his intellectual nature.

Taurus Girl and Pisces Guy

On the plus side: The Pisces guy is always a bit needy, and you love being depended on. He'll give you lots of hugs and kisses to make you feel safe and secure.

The negatives: If you do things for him when he is in one of his oh-woe-is-me moods, he might not notice your efforts. You'll never say no, even if you are feeling a bit resentful about it.

Making the most of it: Your Piscean will be so relieved that you are there to help him through life that he will adore you in return. His moods change like the breeze, so always be there for him to hang on to. He needs lots of reassurance that you love him.

GEMINI GIRL

Gemini Girl and Aries Guy

On the plus side: You are both witty and you love to try new things. Aries' male energy makes you feel safe. He loves your flirty nature.

The negatives: You have a detachment about love that the Aries guy doesn't. He may throw a temper tantrum over this occasionally. You're also intellectually more demanding. Is the guy smart enough to stick around?

Making the most of it: Let him lead and take it in stride. When you need time off, be discreet about it. As long as you don't flaunt it in his face, he'll let you have your space.

Gemini Girl and Taurus Guy

On the plus side: You are friendly, he is down-to-earth. You're both interested in each other—until you see some of the other stuff.

The negatives: You're always on the move, restlessly looking for the new cool experience. He is a creature of habit and likes to stay close to home.

Making the most of it: Slow down and really listen to what he is saying and you'll bring out his love and humor. Taureans like to hold on to everything very tightly. This is deadly to a freedom-loving Gemini. You can lose interest if he doesn't keep up with your lightning speed.

Gemini Girl and Gemini Guy

On the plus side: Two Geminis make the most popular, hip, and cool couple. You'll always have an exciting time together.

The negatives: Because neither of you wants to dive too deeply into anything, this pairing can stay on the shallow side. You also both get too easily distracted by others.

Making the most of it: Make sure you two hang out

with friends who are a mix of other signs—you need stabilizing energy and you're not going to get it from each other. Also, don't make rash decisions about the relationship. Force yourself to be contemplative even though it goes against the grain.

Gemini Girl and Cancer Guy

On the plus side: You are attracted by his caring, tender side. He likes the way you make him feel comfortable.

The negatives: You'll soon find that whatever attention you give him is not enough. His mood swings will drive you up the wall.

Making the most of it: If you want to comfort the Cancer, you're going to have to stop being so friendly to the rest of the world and spend more time at home. But he'll need to let you go out and be yourself, because you get bored without constant activity.

Gemini Girl and Leo Guy

On the plus side: You love his royal self-esteem. He loves your outgoing personality. He'll love to show you off.

The negatives: You can both compete for others' attention. As long as you are lighthearted about this, it might be fun. At some point, he'll make demands on you that you find dumb.

Making the most of it: Keep it light and playful.

This should be easy most of the time, but if your Leo tries to pull you into one of his bad moods, you can get snippy and return the fire. Use your sense of humor to get over it quickly. Don't try to steal the spotlight—there is plenty of attention to go around.

Gemini Girl and Virgo Guy

On the plus side: You're both ruled by Mercury, making you an intelligent and quick-thinking couple.

The negatives: He is reserved and hypercritical. He thinks you are flighty and shallow. You just find him boring.

Making the most of it: Combine your smarts and put your energies into projects or hobbies that Gemini creates and Virgo can make a reality. Be careful that you don't say anything to hurt his feelings. He needs to accept you as you are and not try to change you—that's a big sticking point that's not going to go away.

Gemini Girl and Libra Guy

On the plus side: You both love to hang out and talk about everything from politics to music to clothes.

The negatives: You both like to have a good time and will spend whatever it takes to do that. Geminis and Libras hate the dark side of life, so you both may avoid looking at the bills.

Making the most of it: This is a good fit. You love to travel and do new things, go to parties, and talk a lot.

As long as you stay busy and true to yourselves, you'll have no problem. Both the Twins and the Scales have this out-of-sight, out-of-mind attitude, so watch that you don't get too busy with other things.

Gemini Girl and Scorpio Guy

On the plus side: You are both creative and have tons of energy to burn. Unfortunately, that's all there is.

The negatives: You are too friendly and open for Scorpio's jealous, secretive nature. He'll make a lot of demands for your time, attention, and affection.

Making the most of it: Give him lots of reassurances that you care about him. Don't flirt with other guys when you are with him. In return, your Scorpio has got to let you leave the house without sending a private investigator after you. When you do go off on your own, make sure you leave enough time for him so that he doesn't feel left out.

Gemini Girl and Sagittarius Guy

On the plus side: You're both on a restless search for new experiences and adventures. You'll be great friends as well as sweethearts.

The negatives: You both act too quickly for your own good sometimes, and this can be the downfall of the relationship.

Making the most of it: Once you like each other, try

to take it one step at a time. Both Geminis and Sags like to hop, skip, and jump through life, so you'll have to tame these energies if you want to stay together. Make sure to tell each other how you feel, or show it—neither of you is very good at that, either.

Gemini Girl and Capricorn Guy

On the plus side: Capricorn will enjoy your attention as long as you talk about what's important to him and praise him for his hard work.

The negatives: He is way too serious for you and has a very closed wallet. You'll try to bring out his social side but will get blown off in the process.

Making the most of it: Let him help you organize and run your pet projects. Get used to being with him and having to keep yourself busy at the same time. Bringing a book, journal, or cell phone over to his house is a good idea. Eventually his dry attitude toward life could drive you away.

Gemini Girl and Aquarius Guy

On the plus side: You are both open-minded, quick thinkers who love to try new things.

The negatives: You can be very unpredictable, even more so than your Aquarian. He can get a bit jealous or obstinate at times, something you are going to have to deal with whether you like it or not.

Making the most of it: This is a no-brainer. Read

the newspapers and check out cool Web sites—that'll give you something to do together and something to talk about. Be friends first. That'll give you a chance to get to know each other, and then the whole thing will feel very natural to you.

Gemini Girl and Pisces Guy

On the plus side: You are both adaptable to new situations and care about other people.

The negatives: He is way too sensitive and emotional for you. Everything you do and say has the potential to hurt his tender feelings. He'll enjoy going out with you for a spontaneous adventure as much as he enjoys a flu shot.

Making the most of it: Give your Pisces lots of love and attention. Never take for granted that he knows where he stands with you, especially when you are going off on your own. Call him just to check in and let him know what you've been up to.

CANCER GIRL

Cancer Girl and Aries Guy

On the plus side: You'll love his way of diving right into love.

The negatives: You don't like Aries' forceful ways. He won't be able to handle your moods and your need for emotional security. There'll be too many emotional outbursts over small things.

Making the most of it: This is a near-impossible task. Don't brood if all your Aries wants you to do is tag along on his daily adventures. Don't hold on when he wants to go, and don't get jealous if he stays away too long. Find other friends who are more like you to hang out with when he's gone.

Cancer Girl and Taurus Guy

On the plus side: You are both creatures of habit. Your Taurus guy will make you feel secure, and you'll dote on him as only a Cancer can.

The negatives: You can both get moody and shut down when your feelings are hurt. You're both very sensitive and take the other's actions very personally.

Making the most of it: Hug and kiss your Taurus often. Show him how much you love him by making him cookies and little remembrances. Make the first move and spend as much time as you want with him—he loves the emotional, clingy type. Let him know you appreciate all the things he does for you.

Cancer Girl and Gemini Guy

On the plus side: The Gemini wit will inspire you and make you laugh. At first you'll attract Gemini with your empathy.

The negatives: You get attached to your sweetheart, while he keeps things too superficial for your emotional tastes. You'll never feel completely safe because you'll never quite know where you stand with a Gemini guy.

Making the most of it: If you want to keep him, then always stay a bit detached. Be busy with your own stuff and only see him occasionally. Go to parties and do group events together—just make sure you spend time talking to other people and you don't get jealous when he flirts with other girls. It's just his way.

Cancer Girl and Cancer Guy

On the plus side: You are both clingy, emotional types. You understand what each other needs.

The negatives: You can get pretty moody by yourself. Add another Cancer and you're in for double trouble. You might feel like you're giving all the support and not getting enough in return.

Making the most of it: Once you get to know him, don't use your insight against him or this will deteriorate into something bad. Set firm boundaries so you don't feel taken advantage of and tell him when you need something that you are not getting.

Cancer Girl and Leo Guy

On the plus side: You love all of that testosterone. He loves to be coddled and adored.

The negatives: He attracts a lot of girls and that can

get you jealous. He can be bossy and arrogant at times, which bugs you, especially when it's you he's bossing.

Making the most of it: Give this guy a long leash—he's popular and outgoing and that's not going to change. He loves to hear how great he is, so give him lots of compliments. He'll cheer you up when you're down, but don't be too needy. He's a little too independent for that.

Cancer Girl and Virgo Guy

On the plus side: You are both security-conscious and reserved. Hold on to Virgo guy through your emotional flip-flops. He's a rock and will do anything he can to help.

The negatives: When you are moody and you just want to be alone, he tries to tell you what to do. When you don't respond, he becomes a nag. Ouch.

Making the most of it: Give him lots of love. When he knows he is appreciated it'll make him work harder to please you. Don't attack him when you are brooding. If he wants to fix you, it's just his way of trying to help. Gently tell him to cool it when you've had enough.

Cancer Girl and Libra Guy

On the plus side: At first you'll be very attracted to Libra guy's charm and grace. That'll quickly fade when you realize that's all there is to him.

The negatives: You want a real connection, but he

is just too light and airy. He'll run away at the first sign of one of your famous Cancerian moods.

Making the most of it: Keep this to parties and group social activities. You can add an occasional trip to the mall or dinner, but only when you are in a great mood. Don't show him your deep emotional side and always play hard-to-get.

Cancer Girl and Scorpio Guy

On the plus side: When you fall in love, you both want to stick to your sweethearts like glue. You'll really get into each other's emotions and intuitively understand one another perfectly.

The negatives: You two can each get into some pretty bad moods, and neither of you is reserved about it. You're also prone to jealous fits, deserved or not.

Making the most of it: This is an easy formula. Share everything with each other and do everything together. Call him at odd hours just to tell him how you feel about him. When you are angry at him, don't go out of your way to make him mad or jealous.

Cancer Girl and Sagittarius Guy

On the plus side: With his friendly manner, Sag guy can put you at ease and open you to new ways of thinking.

The negatives: He is a restless, noncommittal pleasure seeker. You can only feel secure when there is a binding contract, but he is way too elusive for you.

Making the most of it: Always be friendly when you are around him and keep your emotions in check. Never be needy; in fact, let him plan things or just go with the flow and see where it takes you. If he thinks you are asking for a commitment, even for one date, he gets squeamish.

Cancer Girl and Capricorn Guy

On the plus side: You like the security that Capricorn guy provides. He likes someone to dote on him and appreciate all his hard work.

The negatives: He is emotionally cool and only interested in things that involve work. You are way too emotional and people-oriented.

Making the most of it: Become part of his work and he'll pay lots of attention to you. Make him special dinners where you can just talk and focus on each other. If you're not getting what you need from him, don't sulk in the corner—talk to him about it. Tell him how great he is; that'll warm him up for a little while.

Cancer Girl and Aquarius Guy

On the plus side: When you first meet him, you'll find him upbeat and friendly. He'll like your natural ability to understand him.

The negatives: He's a bit of a loner. Cancer's need to connect will never be satisfied by his constant detachment. Your play-it-safe attitude clashes with his adventurous side.

Making the most of it: First, don't dote on your Aquarius. Don't constantly hug him and tell him how much you care, and don't expect those kinds of displays from him. Give him the time he needs to do his own thing and don't ask him where he's been when he returns. Read a lot about new technology, politics, and the world and talk to him about it.

Cancer Girl and Pisces Guy

On the plus side: You two are the most psychic signs, so you'll understand each other perfectly. He'll love how you take care of him.

The negatives: You both have mood swings that shift with the tides. When you are both in a bad mood it can get pretty gloomy. Neither one of you can listen to the other; you'll just want to complain about yourself.

Making the most of it: Just be yourselves. Spend time talking about your spiritual beliefs and how to help the world. Tell each other when something is on your mind. Don't pretend it doesn't matter.

LEO GIRL

Leo Girl and Aries Guy

On the plus side: You have great chemistry from the first minute. Whether you're hanging out at a party or wandering around town, it's one big adventure.

The negatives: You've both cornered the market on grabbing attention, and sharing it might be difficult. To you, some of the things he does are too gross. You are far more dignified than him.

Making the most of it: You're going to have to let him make some of the decisions and learn to follow along. Do a lot of things separately that you can control. Then when you come together, it'll be easier to share the lead role. Get this down and it'll be perfect.

Leo Girl and Taurus Guy

On the plus side: You like to have a lot of admirers around, and he is a very loyal friend.

The negatives: He won't like your tendency to control. He'll simply dig in his heels and get stubborn over it. This'll be a bad scene.

Making the most of it: Work on giving him some space to make his own decisions. Don't challenge him when you both want to do different things. You both like to be told how special and fabulous you are, so you'll have to focus on giving that attention rather than getting it.

Leo Girl and Gemini Guy

On the plus side: Gemini has a great sense of humor and is always up for trying new things. You love his flirtatious nature.

The negatives: You can get jealous when he becomes

too friendly with other people. He takes too much attention away from where it really belongs—to you.

Making the most of it: Read the hippest magazines and Web sites, then when you are together you can talk to him about everything. Let him chat as much as he wants. Make every day a new experience and he'll stick with you. If he gets bored, he may wander.

Leo Girl and Cancer Guy

On the plus side: You love how he showers you with attention. Your cheery energy is a great antidote for his moods.

The negatives: His devotion can be smothering. If you try to dominate him he can brood and sulk.

Making the most of it: With you, life is performance art. Tone down the drama a notch before it overwhelms him. Instead of always going out, plan some quiet evenings at home. Tell him about everything that happens and how you feel about it. Hang all over him—he'll love it, though you may not like that role.

Leo Girl and Leo Guy

On the plus side: The ultimate royal couple! You two will create a grand romance to rival the fairy tales.

The negatives: Who is going to call the shots? Who is going to be center stage? Long-term, this relationship has some big competition issues.

Making the most of it: Have separate groups of friends whom you can each call your own. Practice sharing the lead: One day you plan the date; let him do it the next time. Make sure you both have equal time as the star.

Leo Girl and Virgo Guy

On the plus side: He'll be one of your fans if you let him organize your life. Virgo guy loves to be needed, and you can always use help.

The negatives: He can nitpick till you roar. He turns his nose up at your dramatic excesses.

Making the most of it: You can't drag him to parties and put him on display like you can with other signs. This guy needs security, not a good time. Invite everyone for a dinner and prepare the food together. If he tells you there is a better way to do something, take it lightly.

Leo Girl and Libra Guy

On the plus side: Libra guy charms you senseless, loves a good party, and will let you be the leader. Sounds like heaven!

The negatives: His casual attitude toward love and flirtatious ways can make you a little miffed if he flaunts it. You might run through all your money together, and neither of you likes to work that much.

Making the most of it: Take him to the mall; Libra

guys actually like to shop for nice things. He loves to play the role of popular boyfriend, so show him off at big events. Avoid messy sporting events: He prefers intellectual activities, and he doesn't like to get dirty!

Leo Girl and Scorpio Guy

On the plus side: Well, hmmmm—other than an initial attraction, there isn't much to talk about here.

The negatives: You don't understand his intense, brooding nature. He thinks your flamboyant displays are over-the-top.

Making the most of it: This is an impossible task. You'll have to follow him around and deal with his bad moods, his jealousy and mild paranoia.

Leo Girl and Sagittarius Guy

On the plus side: Sags make the best friends in the zodiac. He is so full of fun and adventure, you'll have the best time with him.

The negatives: Archers are difficult to pin down, so he might not be as available to you as you'd like.

Making the most of it: Happy-go-lucky, your Sagittarian will gladly follow you around, so always plan exciting things to do together. Don't expect too much; he cringes when people want things from him. If he disappears for a few days, don't get jealous and ask him too many questions. That'll turn him off. You just have to trust him.

Leo Girl and Capricorn Guy

On the plus side: His reserve intrigues you at first—but every guy intrigues you, so that's nothing big.

The negatives: He is cold and stingy. In addition to that, he looks down on your playful warmth and extravagant spending.

Making the most of it: He is a workaholic. The only way you'd keep this going is to get him to work for you. Give him lots of praise for his efforts and don't expect any in return. Don't try to dominate him, either, because he'll get mad and then just keep it to himself.

Leo Girl and Aquarius Guy

On the plus side: Aquarians are unconventional and energetic. You like a lively love life and this guy fits the bill.

The negatives: He is too independent to follow you around. He'll let you know exactly how much he resents it, and that will hurt your Leo pride.

Making the most of it: You are much more people-oriented than him, so you need to give your Aquarian a lot of space. He needs to do his own thing, and only he knows what that is. Let him be his oddball self; don't judge his actions or try to get him to change in order to fit in better with your crowd.

Leo Girl and Pisces Guy

On the plus side: The Pisces guy is attracted to all your energy. The wishy-washy Fish is all too happy to have you to lead him wherever you want to go.

The negatives: He is way too mushy, emotional, and clingy for you. You want to go out and have a good time, and he just wants to stay home, close to Mother.

Making the most of it: Take him to parties where he knows a lot of the other guests so that he will feel comfortable. Plan quiet evenings at cool places so you can both have a good time. Listen to him when he needs to talk, and give him lots of hugs.

VIRGO GIRL

Virgo Girl and Aries Guy

On the plus side: At first glance, you are attracted to his straightforward approach. That's pretty much where it ends.

The negatives: He is too crass for your reserved tastes. He'll try to pull you out of your shell and will just end up making it worse.

Making the most of it: Get used to following him around and doing risky, stupid things for his enjoyment. Organize his closets, but don't try to tell him what to wear or he'll get annoyed.

Virgo Girl and Taurus Guy

On the plus side: You both love sweethearts who are down-to-earth and like to have your fun close to home.

The negatives: This pairing might become all work and no play. You can get a bit critical, and he can be pretty stubborn about things. That'll make for some impassable obstacles.

Making the most of it: Taurus guys have a lot of stamina, so suggest hikes in the park or bike rides. He also loves to eat. Cook him a meal and make a big dessert. Control your urge to tell him what to do, and definitely don't try to fix him. He is a sensitive guy under that Taurean bravado and doesn't like to be bossed around.

Virgo Girl and Gemini Guy

On the plus side: Your active minds are always working, sizing things up and analyzing them.

The negatives: He is way too immature, always looking to joke and play. You have important things to do, and he'll never take you seriously.

Making the most of it: Watch the same TV shows and movies, read the same magazines and books. Then at least when you're both in a critical mood you can pick them apart instead of each other. Focus your energies into the same hobbies; he is a writer/actor, you are the producer. Give him a lot of freedom. He's always going to keep things light, and you'll never get him to calm down, so don't even try.

Virgo Girl and Cancer Guy

On the plus side: He's a sweet, sensitive guy who touches your heart. His affectionate personality makes you feel special.

The negatives: His moods will bring out the critical side of your personality. He doesn't like being told what's wrong with him, and that'll make the moods worse.

Making the most of it: Skip the big parties. The more time you spend with each other, the better. Plan walks on the beach and picnics in the park. When it comes to relationships, neither of you is great at sharing your deepest feelings. When you are upset, instead of shutting down, talk about what's bothering you.

Virgo Girl and Leo Guy

On the plus side: You're attracted to his lion-sized personality. He's fascinated by your reserved nature and wants to know the girl behind the mask.

The negatives: He always puts himself on display, while you think this is completely overindulgent. You try to rein him in and that's when things get sour.

Making the most of it: The only way to keep this guy is to be hands-off. Tell him how fabulous he is, but don't try to tell it like it is. His huge ego leaves no room for criticism of any kind. Don't try to plan things, either—he'll feel like you are trying to control him.

Virgo Girl and Virgo Guy

On the plus side: You're both great at doing special things for your sweethearts. Little things count a lot, and no one else has the detailed nature of a Virgo.

The negatives: Virgos tend to be overly critical of each other, telling the other what to do and how to do it. This doesn't sit well with either of you.

Making the most of it: Let your Virgo guy do nice things for you, accept them, and let him know how much you appreciate him. Never take him for granted or tell him how you would do things. If he does that to you, don't take it personally—it's just his way of loving you.

Virgo Girl and Libra Guy

On the plus side: He'll coax you out of your shell and make you feel beautiful. You'll be inspired to do things for him.

The negatives: All he wants to do is go to parties; he doesn't seem to have any serious goals. If you try to straighten him up, he'll just shut down.

Making the most of it: The only way this is going to work is if you just have fun with him. Go shopping or out to dinner, but it's better to include other friends as well because if you turn the conversation to important things, he won't know how to respond. Don't expect too much from him.

Virgo Girl and Scorpio Guy

On the plus side: Scorpio guy likes to get to know his sweetheart to the core. All this energy directed your way makes you feel warm and fuzzy.

The negatives: You could do without his secretive ways. His purely emotional reactions can drive analytical Virgo bonkers. You like to think in facts, not fiction.

Making the most of it: He needs someone to keep his volatile nature steady, so always be available for him. Listen to what he is *not* saying for a clue to how he really feels. Anticipate what he needs and do it in advance. All this is easy for earthy Virgo—just make sure you compromise when it comes to steering the ship.

Virgo Girl and Sagittarius Guy

On the plus side: There is an initial friendship, but honestly, the Sag will only stick around as long as it suits him.

The negatives: The serious, quiet Virgo looks down on Sag's restless, risk-taking ways. You think he'll never get anywhere in life, and you don't want to hang out long enough to pick up the pieces.

Making the most of it: With him you have to have a live-and-let-live attitude. Don't try to change him or settle him down. The minute he senses your displeasure at his frivolous ways he'll make a joke and dance away. Let him take you on one of his spontaneous adventures—you may have some unexpected fun.

Virgo Girl and Capricorn Guy

On the plus side: Your Capricorn guy appreciates the way you set goals and accomplish things that are important to you. He is also ambitious and likes to be in a stable relationship.

The negatives: This can get a little boring. Neither sign is fun-loving or adventurous in any way. You'll have to work at creating romance.

Making the most of it: When your Capricorn sweetheart does things for you, always let him know how much you appreciate him. Respect his goals and interests and tell him about yours. Work is very important to both of you; helping each other complete projects will give you something to do together.

Virgo Girl and Aquarius Guy

On the plus side: Since you're both logical thinkers, you'll get along well enough for a first conversation.

The negatives: His offbeat way of doing things drives you crazy; you find fault with everything. You think his ideas are quite unrealistic.

Making the most of it: Since he's a thinker and you

are a doer, you could follow him around and put his schemes into action. Don't try to get him to think in your terms and don't try to lead him down your road, or he will only get resentful. He needs freedom, so don't feel rejected when he seems distant.

Virgo Girl and Pisces Guy

On the plus side: Your Pisces guy will romance you right off your feet. Practical Virgo helps the waffling Fish to find its way.

The negatives: You think his fantasy world is an unnecessary indulgence. His sensitive personality won't be able to stand up to your perfectionistic Virgo standards.

Making the most of it: You can make a go of this by helping your Pisces when he needs it. But be sure to stop before it becomes too much for him and he drowns in your chilly criticisms. Also, try hanging out in his reality once in a while—it's fun to be in fantasyland.

LIBRA GIRL

Libra Girl and Aries Guy

On the plus side: You're attracted to those fun bursts of Aries energy. He is easily charmed by you, and you can always add another admirer to the list.

The negatives: He says and does things that you find

awkward and thoughtless. His tantrums can throw off your fine Libran balance.

Making the most of it: This is definitely doable if you follow some simple steps. If he wants to go out on a new adventure and you're not up for it, let him go alone, but reassure him you'll be there when he gets back. When you are at a party, pay extra attention to him so he knows how special he is.

Libra Girl and Taurus Guy

On the plus side: You both value art and beauty. You two even appreciate fine food: You like it expensive and he just likes a lot of it!

The negatives: No amount of money is too much for Libra to spend on fun, and your Taurus guy thinks that is too extravagant. On the other hand, you think he's boring.

Making the most of it: See a lot of concerts and theater together. Take a painting class. Stay at home and order in some food from a fancy restaurant. Give him hugs, stroke his hair—these things tell him you care about him. Don't flirt with other people in front of him unless you want to make him upset.

Libra Girl and Gemini Guy

On the plus side: He's smart, popular, and he's got a sense of humor. He'll appreciate your intellect and your good looks.

The negatives: You both talk a lot and charm other people into doing your dirty work. You also both get bored quickly and move on.

Making the most of it: Have plenty of parties and fun activities planned; he likes constant action. Talk to him about all the trendy restaurants you can go to together. Take a trip to the mall to check out the latest clothes and cool decorations. If you stay at home, make sure there is a computer or TV handy to keep your minds working.

Libra Girl and Cancer Guy

On the plus side: He is approachable and kind. He'll listen to your problems better than anyone else.

The negatives: You want to go out and have some fun. He just wants to stay at home and act like a dud. He needs more cooing and cuddling than you're willing to give.

Making the most of it: Go out for high tea; something elegant for you and sentimental for him. If you bring him to a party, make sure he knows some people there and hang out with him a lot so he doesn't feel left out or rejected.

Libra Girl and Leo Guy

On the plus side: You just love all that luxurious Leo bravado. He likes to have a smart, sassy, and well-dressed Libra on his arm.

The negatives: He can get jealous if you're too friendly with other guys. When mad he can throw quite a tantrum, and that can tip your scales.

Making the most of it: Just have the best time you can and don't worry about a thing. Tell him often how cute and fabulous he is. Let him take the lead, and when you need your space, be graceful about it and don't challenge him.

Libra Girl and Virgo Guy

On the plus side: You can use your subtle charm to get this guy to do all the little messy things you really dislike.

The negatives: He'll do them, but he'll also try to fix you up in the process.

Making the most of it: Be serious around him. He is a bit reserved and doesn't like to hang around people who are too casual. Tell him you admire his work and appreciate all he does for you. He won't let you know, but he needs more emotional support than he lets on. This may sometimes be more than you're willing to give.

Libra Girl and Libra Guy

On the plus side: You are so much alike that you'll love going to the same parties and planning exciting and expensive dates.

The negatives: Too much alike can be a bad thing as

well. If you spend a lot of time together, the relationship can get stale.

Making the most of it: Do fun things together, but also have some other friends and interests to keep you busy outside of him. Read up on the latest politics and fashion trends—that way you'll always have something current to talk about. If you get bored, take a little time away from each other.

Libra Girl and Scorpio Guy

On the plus side: He'll give you plenty of attention and you love that. He is intensely creative and you understand the artist in him.

The negatives: He is possessive, jealous, and controlling. Pleasure-seeking Libra will have problems with him at every turn.

Making the most of it: If you want him, you can keep him, but you'll have to do a few things first. When you are out and about, don't get too friendly with anyone else. If you do talk to other people, let him know that he is the only guy for you. If you need your space, tell him where you're going and when you'll be back.

Libra Girl and Sagittarius Guy

On the plus side: You like his friendly, no-nonsense personality. Your charm, wit, and complete freedom are everything he adores in a girl.

The negatives: You're both easily distracted and can lose interest rather quickly.

Making the most of it: Plan fun little adventures to keep your Sag's attention. Play pool, take a trip to an amusement park—you can even go to a playground. Read up on politics and philosophy and talk to him about it. Do lots of things in groups so there are other people around to have fun with.

Libra Girl and Capricorn Guy

On the plus side: A Capricorn is one of those guys you want hanging around when you need something done. They love to work.

The negatives: He thinks your casual attitude is frivolous. He also disses your love and affection.

Making the most of it: If you want to stick with a Capricorn, you've got your work cut out for you. You'll have to show him that he needs you and then get him to work for it. He doesn't understand people who just like to have fun, so make sure you show him your serious side. Create enterprising activities to do together so that your energies are focused on the same thing.

Libra Girl and Aquarius Guy

On the plus side: You two have so much in common. You both like to keep yourself busy with friends. You are creative and care about the world.

The negatives: You'll be fine as long as you don't mind his stubbornness and occasional jealousy.

Making the most of it: This is an easy formula. Be good friends, do fun things together, and occasionally do something to make the world a better place. When either of you needs some space, just ask for it. You might have to tell your Aquarian what you're up to so he doesn't start to think the worst.

Libra Girl and Pisces Guy

On the plus side: You both love to be in love. You're also into creating a bit of fantasy wherever you go.

The negatives: Your Pisces guy will always need your help and your constant affection. After a while this will be suffocating.

Making the most of it: Keep other friends around so that they can take some of that Piscean neediness off your hands. Plan to do quiet things with your guy that are around the neighborhood, since Pisces like to isolate themselves. Talk to him about your feelings, give him lots of hugs and kisses, and listen to him when he wants to talk.

SCORPIO GIRL

Scorpio Girl and Aries Guy

On the plus side: You are both strong-willed and full of energy. At first this may seem like a great match.

The negatives: You both want to be in the driver's seat and are willing to fight for it. He is too wild and open for your mysterious makeup. You need someone more subtle.

Making the most of it: You might be able to prolong the agony if you surrendered control of things most of the time. You'd also have to pretend you like being the focus of all his energy.

Scorpio Girl and Taurus Guy

On the plus side: You both have a lot of willpower. Whatever you are doing, neither of you will quit.

The negatives: You are both possessive and jealous. Scorpio is intense; you are obstinate. This makes for fireworks you don't want to see.

Making the most of it: As long as you two are on the same team you'll be okay. This might sound weird, but if you have a common enemy or common goals, you'll have a better shot at getting along. Be affectionate and let him know how wonderful he is. Don't challenge him. Curb your brooding when you don't get what you want.

Scorpio Girl and Gemini Guy

On the plus side: This charming, chatty guy will disarm your defenses. He'll want to get to know that secretive side of you better.

The negatives: You'll find his emotional detachment strange. When you tighten the reins in response, he'll only become more restless and uninterested.

Making the most of it: This might work for a time if you drop the possessiveness and brooding. Gemini guy likes his freedom. He is light and cheerful and refuses to let anyone drag him down. Don't compromise yourself to keep him. He probably won't stick around for long anyway.

Scorpio Girl and Cancer Guy

On the plus side: He loves your possessiveness. You love how he intuitively knows what you need without your asking for it.

The negatives: You both can get jealous and moody, so there are bound to be some arguments.

Making the most of it: Hang all over this guy and he'll hang all over you in return. This makes you both feel safe and secure. Both Scorpios and Cancers are secretive; use your sixth sense to figure out how he is feeling and he'll naturally do the same with you.

Scorpio Girl and Leo Guy

On the plus side: At first, you're attracted to each other's energy.

The negatives: You think his daily drama is way too showy, and you really dislike the way he spends money on himself.

Making the most of it: You like to control; Leos like

to dominate. The only way you're going to make a go of this is to enjoy following him around. If he takes the lead and you get seething mad inside (like Scorpios do), you're just going to explode eventually.

Scorpio Girl and Virgo Guy

On the plus side: You both take love seriously and make deep commitments to people.

The negatives: Virgo guys aren't the huggy-kissy type you like so much. He also relies on fact and you go by gut feelings.

Making the most of it: Find out his goals, talents, and interests and tell him how much you admire him. Talk about how you want to heal the world and make it a better place. Do cool things that are meaningful to both of you—sit on a swing and discuss life or go to poetry readings.

Scorpio Girl and Libra Guy

On the plus side: Libras are affectionate. You'll love the way he pays extra attention to you.

The negatives: Under all that love he is flirty and shallow. You need more out of love than a handsome face.

Making the most of it: This can work for a little while if you give him a long leash. He needs to be friendly with everyone and go out a lot, nothing you're particularly interested in. Don't expect a lot of heavy-duty emotions. Talk to him about politics and equality in the world. Cut out your jealous tendencies.

Scorpio Girl and Scorpio Guy

On the plus side: You are attracted to each other's intensity. Nothing scares a Scorpio, not even another Scorpio.

The negatives: You're both used to being a vortex of energy and having everything revolve around you. Tug-of-war is fun, but it'll be a constant struggle after a while.

Making the most of it: First off, you must have your own group of friends and separate hobbies. You can spend a lot of time together, but make sure you each have your own areas to focus on. Don't try to take over each other's jobs. Learn to give in and don't make everything a challenge.

Scorpio Girl and Sagittarius Guy

On the plus side: Scorpios and Sagittarians make fast friends. He'll gladly let you lead, but after a short time you might have a problem keeping his attention.

The negatives: You like to get deep into your sweetheart's soul. He is so flighty and noncommittal that you are left wondering if he *has* a soul.

Making the most of it: Stay the best of friends. Accept him unconditionally—that means letting him leave without asking him where he's going and how long he'll be gone. If your feelings are hurt, let him know with humor and lightness (if you can).

Scorpio Girl and Capricorn Guy

On the plus side: He loves your drive and ambition. You'll both do anything to achieve your goals.

The negatives: You need more affectionate displays than he'll give you. You might butt heads once in a while when he is in one of his commanding moods, but you'll usually win.

Making the most of it: Appreciate all his hard work and he'll always do things for you. Since he's the kind of guy who can get miffed and not show it, make sure to use your intuition to find out how he really feels. Getting possessive will make him feel like he's important.

Scorpio Girl and Aquarius Guy

On the plus side: He'll go along with you, at least for a time, so it'll be fun while it lasts.

The negatives: He is way too friendly and independent. No matter how much he likes you, he'll never really be able to shower you with love and affection.

Making the most of it: You do have some things in common, and if you stick to those things you might be able to keep him interested. Don't expect him to drop his friends and hobbies for you and don't try to hold on too tight.

Scorpio Girl and Pisces Guy

On the plus side: Deeply emotional and intuitive, you form a lasting bond. Two water signs bring out the best in each other.

The negatives: When you are upset you have a stinging way with words, and that can hurt the supersensitive Pisces. You can both brood in silence rather than fix a problem.

Making the most of it: This perfect pair doesn't need much advice. Smother each other with affection. Hang out all the time but don't forget your friends and responsibilities. Surprise him with love notes and meaningful gifts that'll remind him of you.

SAGITTARIUS GIRL

Sagittarius Girl and Aries Guy

On the plus side: You are both outgoing and friendly. You also love a good party and an exciting adventure.

The negatives: You do have a temper and aren't afraid to let it fly, so there are bound to be some fiery displays.

Making the most of it: Challenge your Aries to a game of pool or basketball. You both love to do new things. The only hitch: Your Aries guy likes to take the lead, so making good-natured suggestions will go further than trying to plan things on your own. Just be your fun self and you'll have no problems keeping this one.

Sagittarius Girl and Taurus Guy

On the plus side: You'll like his easygoing personality; you can always use a new friend.

The negatives: He is a slow-moving creature of habit. You like to be on the move and constantly try new things. This mixes like oil and water.

Making the most of it: Since Taurus guys are loyal, you might get one to stick around until you get bored with him. Here's how: Go with him to his favorite hangouts. Talk to him about his goals and dreams. When Friday night comes, let him decide what to do and how to do it.

Sagittarius Girl and Gemini Guy

On the plus side: You are both chatty, lively, and fun to be around. There is nothing that you won't do together.

The negatives: You can both tell it like it is, and if you're at odds, that may not be pretty.

Making the most of it: Go to parties. Be creative when planning your adventures. Read up on cool travel magazines and Web sites so that you'll always have something new to talk about. Hanging out with other people will keep it fresh, but watch the flirting—you can easily end up with other people.

Sagittarius Girl and Cancer Guy

On the plus side: Cancer guy is a great listener and would love to find out all about your travels and adventures.

The negatives: He is clingy, whiny, and nagging. Your idea of love doesn't include being totally consumed by someone, thank you.

Making the most of it: Why would you want to keep this going when there are better pairings out there? Whatever your answer, there are things you can do. Bake him cookies. Hang out with him and do nothing. Give him constant displays of affection.

Sagittarius Girl and Leo Guy

On the plus side: You hit it off right away and continue to have fun. You know how to soothe your Leo no matter what mood he's in.

The negatives: You like to go off and do your own thing. If his ego gets hurt, no one roars louder than a Lion.

Making the most of it: Plan many parties and dinners for friends so you guys can hang out and your Leo can rule the roost. Do fun things together outdoors or in public places; that way your Leo can show off. When you want to tell him something important, think before you speak and be as tactful as you can.

Sagittarius Girl and Virgo Guy

On the plus side: Since you both have sharp minds, you'll enjoy a good conversation.

The negatives: Virgo guy will try to keep your feet firmly planted on the ground, all the while telling you better ways to live your life. He has no idea what he's talking about.

Making the most of it: If you need something done or have a group activity to plan, call your Virgo guy. Just make sure there are plenty of other people around to chat and diffuse the energy. He is no adventurer: If you want to hang out with him, expect to do serious things close to home.

Sagittarius Girl and Libra Guy

On the plus side: Libras are so approachable and charming. You'll love how smart he is, too.

The negatives: You are much more of an outdoorsy adventurer than he is, so you might run into some conflicts over how you want to spend your time.

Making the most of it: Keeping this going is easy. Have some good conversations about politics and philosophy. Go to a lot of parties and events where you can both meet people and hang out with friends. Do adventurous artistic things together—go to museums, lectures, and the theater.

Sagittarius Girl and Scorpio Guy

On the plus side: Being an adventuresome Sag, you're always into meeting new people, and this Scorpio guy seems very interesting.

The negatives: He is possessive and emotional and wants to pull you into all that intensity. There is nothing that scares you more than a clingy, brooding guy.

Making the most of it: Go to a funky, out-of-the-way coffee shop and talk to him about important things. You both like to discuss your philosophy and how you look at the world. If his Scorpio energy becomes too much, set your boundaries quietly. Don't run away or hide—he'll find out and get mad.

Sagittarius Girl and Sagittarius Guy

On the plus side: You're both so much alike that you'll be instant friends. Finding someone who understands you so well is thrilling.

The negatives: Since you are both so changeable and easily distracted, this pairing can be unstable.

Making the most of it: Do unto him as you would do unto yourself! Go on many adventures, spend a lot of time with your friends, and when you need your space, take it—you know he won't care. Just make sure to let him know that you really care about him or he might not realize it.

Sagittarius Girl and Capricorn Guy

On the plus side: When you first meet him, you'll want to know what he is hiding under all that reserve.

The negatives: He is focused and driven; he likes to set goals and work to accomplish them. But face it, work is the furthest thing from your mind.

Making the most of it: Take little steps. Your friendly nature will pull him out of his shell—at least temporarily. Just don't expect that he'll be interested in going on a never-ending adventure with you. When he seems too busy for you and you want to go out on your own, just be subtle about it.

Sagittarius Girl and Aquarius Guy

On the plus side: You are attracted to his unconventional personality. He can tell you his oddball ideas about the world and you understand what he's talking about.

The negatives: Between the two of you there isn't an emotional bone in your bodies. Commitment doesn't come easy here.

Making the most of it: Hang out in cutting-edge places that seem futuristic. Spend your time checking out the latest gadgets and technology that'll improve the world. When you want your freedom to go exploring alone, reassure him you'll be back and he'll be fine with it.

Sagittarius Girl and Pisces Guy

On the plus side: Pisces guys are looking for some direction, and friendly Sag is always willing to lend a hand.

The negatives: His clingy, emotional nature will end up weighing you down. When you say what's on your mind, you risk hurting his sensitive nature.

Making the most of it: This has short-term potential, but you'll have to do a few things. Spend time talking to him about your philosophy, spirituality, and beliefs. Give him lots of hugs; send him little notes telling him that you are thinking of him. When he's got a problem, listen to him; then use your sense of humor to lighten things up.

CAPRICORN GIRL

Capricorn Girl and Aries Guy

On the plus side: When you are in the mood for fun, your Aries guy is the wildest in the zodiac.

The negatives: He acts without thinking and then changes his mind midstream. To you this is just plain stupid. You both tend to tell the other what to do.

Making the most of it: Both of you are so sure you are right that this isn't likely to last beyond the first argument. You can try to be less judgmental when he's being shortsighted. You can also practice going with the flow rather than trying to calculate the risks before you go ahead with your plans.

Capricorn Girl and Taurus Guy

On the plus side: You like Taurus's patience and practical thinking. He understands your serious, goal-oriented outlook.

The negatives: You're both pretty strong-willed and can be quite stubborn about getting your way.

Making the most of it: Since you both like to put in good, hard effort to accomplish things, make sure you always have some engaging activities, games, and projects to do together. Make him dinner at home and let your Taurus's earthy romantic side melt your cool edge.

Capricorn Girl and Gemini Guy

On the plus side: The Gemini guy is fun to be around when you're in the mood to party—although you are not in a purely social mood very often.

The negatives: His energy is all over the place, doing five things at once, and he never completes anything. To a well-organized Capricorn, this is irresponsible.

Making the most of it: This may be asking too much of you, but you could have fun if you do a few things. First off, you have to be willing to hang out with your Gemini and forget your serious side (and your judgments about his casual attitude). Then you have to give him freedom to come and go and let him flirt with whomever he pleases without calling him on any of this.

Capricorn Girl and Cancer Guy

On the plus side: A Cancer will listen to you talk about anything and you'll know he cares. Your protective instincts will kick in when you hang out with a Cancer.

The negatives: When you get mad you get cold and domineering. When he gets mad he gets critical and then shuts off.

Making the most of it: If you want to keep him, spend a lot of time letting him know how you feel about him. Don't be too busy or he'll think you're rejecting him. Send him a mushy love note when he least expects it. Make a date to have a quiet dinner at home.

Capricorn Girl and Leo Guy

On the plus side: Leo guys are very outgoing and generous, so he will make you feel at ease.

The negatives: He craves attention and does things to get it that you think are way too desperate. He's too loud, garish, and says things without thinking.

Making the most of it: The key to keeping this guy is to give him the lead role and tell him how great he is all the time. When you get sick of sucking up, it'll be over fast.

Capricorn Girl and Virgo Guy

On the plus side: You both value a safe and secure relationship. You like to spend your time doing things that are important to both of you.

The negatives: Capricorn likes to dominate and that's okay, but your Virgo will take stock of every detail and can pick you apart if he's in a bad mood.

Making the most of it: You can take the dominant role, but always let him know that his opinion counts. Set goals together and focus on them. Let him help you organize and plan your activities. It works.

Capricorn Girl and Libra Guy

On the plus side: He is well-dressed, meticulous, smart, charming. On the outside this is a guy of your heart's desire.

The negatives: After you get to know him a bit, you'll see he is flighty, self-centered, and lazy.

Making the most of it: You'll need to have plenty of time to go to parties and chitchat about all sorts of things. If you are too serious around him, he'll think you're boring and will immediately lose interest.

Capricorn Girl and Scorpio Guy

On the plus side: Scorpio's intensity and possessiveness makes you feel special. You're excited that he wants to totally get to know you inside and out.

The negatives: He can be a bit of a control freak, and even your stubbornness can't match it.

Making the most of it: Use your common drive and ambition and plan some impressive things to do together. If anyone can do the impossible, it's you two. Talk to him about the mysteries of life. He likes public displays of affection, too, so hold his hand or run your fingers through his hair.

Capricorn Girl and Sagittarius Guy

On the plus side: This guy's upbeat and friendly personality picks you up. You feel good around him (at first!).

The negatives: You'll soon learn that his no-strings-attached loyalty isn't good enough for commitment-craving Capricorn.

Making the most of it: This is workable while you are in a playful mood, but you have to make sure that you don't give him all your time and energy and expect to get the same in return. Don't try to demand that he act a certain way and don't feel rejected when he just wants to be friends—he does that with everybody.

Capricorn Girl and Capricorn Guy

On the plus side: You respect his drive, the way he sets his sights on something and doesn't stop until he gets it.

The negatives: Two hardworking Capricorns together

can get dull and dreary. You bring out the worst in each other.

Making the most of it: Since you both like to set out and accomplish things, plan to conquer some exciting challenges. Focus your energies on romance and work hard to achieve that. Keep a positive attitude about your relationship. Let him know how much you appreciate him.

Capricorn Girl and Aquarius Guy

On the plus side: You are attracted to his intelligence and insight right off the bat.

The negatives: He is too much of a visionary for you. You'll think he's missing a few marbles. In return, he'll think you're stodgy and predictable.

Making the most of it: He is a thinker and you are a doer. This will work only if you buy into his improve-the-world mentality and focus on making that vision a reality. Once you have a common goal it'll be easier to see eye to eye. Give him his freedom to be who he wants. Don't try to make him more conventional and presentable.

Capricorn Girl and Pisces Guy

On the plus side: Dreamy Pisces guy adores your stable determination. He also intuitively understands what you need since you're not good at asking for it.

The negatives: He lives in a world far from reality.

His procrastination and constant confusion will have you acting like his drill sergeant.

Making the most of it: Your sensitive Pisces needs you. Just make sure you are always available to lend him your support. You can tell this guy what to do, but make sure you are always kind and remind him how much you love him. He needs more romance than you do, so let him plan some sweet evenings and just enjoy them. His soft side perfectly complements your strength and willpower.

AQUARIUS GIRL

Aquarius Girl and Aries Guy

On the plus side: Finally, a guy who has as much energy as you do and loves to experience new things.

The negatives: He wants to lead all the time, but you don't like to be told what to do.

Making the most of it: Be creative about sharing the leading role. You don't really need to lead—you just don't like to follow all the time, either. Even though you see his macho attitude as a need to get attention, don't challenge him about it. Let him know how great you think he is. Always keep things entertaining and it'll work out well.

Aquarius Girl and Taurus Guy

On the plus side: You'll find the Taurus guy friendly and down-to-earth. There is not much else.

The negatives: He is too slow-moving and traditional for you. As a nonconformist Aquarius, you do everything you can to stray from the course. You'll end up on opposite sides of every issue.

Making the most of it: If you really want to keep this guy, you'll have to curb your adventuresome side. In other words, think inside the box, weigh and measure every detail before acting, and stay close to home. How long can you do this before you get frustrated?

Aquarius Girl and Gemini Guy

On the plus side: You're both smart and witty. You'll enjoy talking to each other about all sorts of things and you'll do a lot of laughing, too.

The negatives: Geminis are a bit flirty and flighty. You both like freedom, but you might find your Gemini's interests going off in too many directions.

Making the most of it: This is a great match, so it should be easy to find things to do together. You're both into the latest computer and phone gadgets, so do a lot of chatting and exploring online. When you're spending quiet time alone, make sure you have enough things to explore close to home.

Aquarius Girl and Cancer Guy

On the plus side: Here's a guy who will listen to you and really understand your feelings. You inspire his adventuresome side—but unfortunately it doesn't come out that often.

The negatives: You want to go out, he wants to stay in. You want to talk about thoughts, he wants to talk about feelings. You want freedom, he wants commitment.

Making the most of it: You might think you like this guy, but to keep him you'll have to hang out with him all the time, tell him everything going on in your life, listen to him complain, and deal with his incredible moods.

Aquarius Girl and Leo Guy

On the plus side: He is a larger-than-life romantic. Once he sets his eyes on you, the rest of the world melts away.

The negatives: He is too into the drama and not enough into the ideas and things that make you who you are. Eventually you'll get sick of Leo's me-me attitude.

Making the most of it: Let your Leo know he's the driver and in return he'll give you enough freedom to do what you want (most of the time). When you're in the mood to change the world, don't go to him. Do it yourself or find one of your other friends. Don't expect him to understand your need to explore new frontiers. According to him, he's all you need.

Aquarius Girl and Virgo Guy

On the plus side: You are both thinkers, so you'll enjoy analyzing things and picking them apart.

The negatives: You like to explore and he likes to stay home. You are outgoing, he is reserved. Too many different goals will make this tough.

Making the most of it: Keeping this guy isn't easy. You'll first have to close your circle of friends to a select few and do more serious-minded things. He needs to see you make a commitment of time and energy to work on things. When you need your freedom, give him something to do that'll keep him busy and his energy focused on the relationship.

Aquarius Girl and Libra Guy

On the plus side: You're both intelligent and fun. You are also big partygoers and have lots of outside interests to keep you busy.

The negatives: Together you are both too independent and freedom-loving for your own good. The needs of the partnership might be neglected.

Making the most of it: You can't lose with a Libra. Take him to jazz concerts and art performances. Talk to him about law, politics, humanity, and righting the wrongs of mankind. Buy him a nice shirt or watch—he appreciates luxury. Be lazy with him and watch high-brow movies all day.

Aquarius Girl and Scorpio Guy

On the plus side: You are attracted to his gutsy energy, his drive and ambition. He likes your humanitarian qualities.

The negatives: When he does something he goes all the way. You always have an elusive detachment in everything you do. This just doesn't mix well.

Making the most of it: Once that initial flirtation is over, the ship starts sinking. Until then, you can do fun and offbeat things with him. Sit on a park bench and talk about the world and the mysteries of life. Play intense mind games such as chess, or better yet, play on the same team against a computer. When he gets possessive or jealous, just deal with it.

Aquarius Girl and Sagittarius Guy

On the plus side: You both thrive on the unusual. You love to explore and experience new things. Aquarians and Sags make the perfect travel buddies.

The negatives: You are both open-minded, but might not believe the same things. You might find your Sag guy has a wandering eye and a short attention span.

Making the most of it: You can take the lead and plan adventures for the mind and spirit. The more creative you are, the longer you'll keep his attention.

He likes to talk about philosophy, law, politics, and travel. Make him laugh a lot and let him take the lead when it comes to talking about the two of you.

Aquarius Girl and Capricorn Guy

On the plus side: You are a visionary. If you manage to win him over with your ambition, you can get him to help you with anything.

The negatives: He has a very set way of thinking and he'll try too hard to make you fit into the mold. You'll give him a piece of your mind and that'll be the end of it.

Making the most of it: There isn't much to make out of this, but you could curb your nonconformist ways for a start. Bring out your quiet, nurturing side and tell him how much you respect him. Plan your evenings at home doing things that are important to both of you.

Aquarius Girl and Aquarius Guy

On the plus side: You are two unconventional, opinionated people who will have a lot of fun together.

The negatives: Your drawbacks are doubled, especially your detachment. No matter how you feel about each other, there will be little emotional connection.

Making the most of it: Taking care of the parties and dates is easy here. Focus on your sweetheart and how you feel about him—don't forget to tell him this! Being apart doesn't affect either of you, but make sure you're not apart more than you are together and that when you are together it is special.

Aquarius Girl and Pisces Guy

On the plus side: The Pisces is a sensitive and romantic guy who will see eye to eye with you on a lot of things.

The negatives: He is too needy for you. Basically, he wants constant affection to soothe his insecurity. You'll get tired of this real fast.

Making the most of it: You can have a good time with him; it just might not last an eternity. Talk about what's wrong with the world and how it should be. Find a place to volunteer and together make the world a better place. Talk to him about your feelings and complain all you want (he is a good listener!). Send him little love notes and e-mails and shower him with affection.

PISCES GIRL

Pisces Girl and Aries Guy

On the plus side: Pisces girl needs a guy who will ride in on a white horse and save the day. His energy fits the bill.

The negatives: Aries have big tempers and a disregard for boundaries. At the end of the day, this can leave you feeling run over.

Making the most of it: At first this might seem great, but the more you get to know him, the more you won't like. Be ready to follow him around on his escapades. Accept his help whether you want to or not. Don't mistake his playfulness for forcefulness. When he criticizes, don't get too upset. Does this sound like something you can do?

Pisces Girl and Taurus Guy

On the plus side: Here's a guy you can lean on through thick and thin. He also likes to do things for you and protect you. Mmmmmm.

The negatives: Sometimes he is too practical for the mystical Pisces. He may get annoyed when you hide in your own reality for too long.

Making the most of it: Create romantic settings close to home to get to know each other. Make him dinner or a picnic. Tell him how much you appreciate him and how strong and determined he is. Ask him to help you with everything, from your finances to fixing up old furniture. That'll make him feel needed and loved.

Pisces Girl and Gemini Guy

On the plus side: You like the Gemini guy because he is so easy to talk to. Gemini guy likes you because you are a great mystery for him to explore.

The negatives: He is too detached and unavailable for you. He doesn't have the deep thoughts and feelings essential to dating a Pisces.

Making the most of it: This can be a short fling if you want to get to know him as much as he'll allow before he runs away. Talk to him about issues, not feelings. Go with him to the hottest restaurants and parties. Don't hang all over him or expect him to do the same. Be friends first and try to always remain a bit elusive—then there will always be something more he wants to know about you.

Pisces Girl and Cancer Guy

On the plus side: You can get all the love and devotion you need from a Cancer. He'll also protect you and give you direction.

The negatives: The two of you can be pretty emotional and needy. Problems come up when you both need coddling at the same time.

Making the most of it: This guy is really perfect for you. Remind him of every anniversary. Every week and month you are together brings another opportunity to give him a love note and a sweet kiss he'll remember forever. Go for romantic boat rides and walks on the beach. Use your intuition to know what he wants, and always follow your instincts.

Pisces Girl and Leo Guy

On the plus side: He is a total romantic. Your first few dates will be the most exciting you've ever had.

The negatives: He is too bold and domineering for

you. If you don't play along, he gets annoyed that you are ruining his game.

Making the most of it: Here's how to make the most of this fling. Let him treat you like a queen. In return, adore him like a king. Follow him around and don't get too whiny about it. Don't make too many emotional demands on him or he'll get all macho and hurt your feelings. Keep a part of yourself hidden so he'll always have something to conquer.

Pisces Girl and Virgo Guy

On the plus side: Virgos are loyal and helpful. Emotional Pisces appreciates his steady nature.

The negatives: Virgo is critical, nitpicky, and constantly trying to change you. He likes to deal in facts and pooh-poohs your feelings and intuition.

Making the most of it: This might work for a little while. Ask him about his goals and tell him about yours. Make sure that you're not too dreamy or he won't believe you. Let him help you organize your life, but make sure he doesn't step all over your boundaries in the process. Trust your intuition.

Pisces Girl and Libra Guy

On the plus side: You are both pleasure-seeking, artistic people. You'll enjoy each other's company (that is, until Pisces wants more).

The negatives: Libra can't deal with your deep emotional needs. He is too selfish and lazy to really take you on.

Making the most of it: You'll be good friends, just don't count on him to give you everything you need. Take him out for expensive desserts. Go shopping for the little artsy decorations you need; plan to spend a lot of money when you're around him. Don't expect his full attention. Don't lay heavy feelings on him.

Pisces Girl and Scorpio Guy

On the plus side: You're both intuitive and emotionally charged. You'll love his intense, commanding energy. This is a special pair.

The negatives: You are very moody water signs and when you have a fight, watch out. His words sting, and you can make him feel pretty guilty about it.

Making the most of it: Just go with the flow and see where it takes you. He'll naturally take charge and that'll make you feel safe. Give him hugs and kisses—he needs a lot of coddling. In fact, you can hang all over him and he'll love it. Tell him how fabulous he is.

Pisces Girl and Sagittarius Guy

On the plus side: At first you think you've found a friendly, available guy. You like his no-nonsense, straightforward approach.

The negatives: He comes and goes when he pleases without caring how you feel. He is so afraid of commitment that you won't feel secure around him.

Making the most of it: You can go on a short adventure with him and love it. Plan things together and use your intuition to know when enough is enough. He's not big on leading, but if he senses you want too much from him, he'll get squeamish. Talk about your philosophy and spirituality. When he disappears, it's nothing personal. That doesn't mean you have to take him back, though.

Pisces Girl and Capricorn Guy

On the plus side: Capricorn guys really know what they want from life and set out to get it and never give up. You love that take-charge attitude.

The negatives: He can get a bit domineering. If your head is too much in the clouds, he'll get annoyed and try to pull you down.

Making the most of it: Even though you seem like opposites, it can really work. Tell him that you admire him a lot; smothering him with your love will make him feel strong. Use your intuition to figure out what he needs. Ask him for his help with projects and he'll work tirelessly for you.

Pisces Girl and Aquarius Guy

On the plus side: When you first meet the visionary Aquarius, you think: Finally, a guy who understands the universe and sees things as I do.

The negatives: After a while you'll see that he has no

emotional connection to anything. He is so busy thinking big that you get lost inside his head.

Making the most of it: You two have enough in common that you can make a go of this. Just don't hold on when it's time to let go. Talk to him about how you want to heal Earth's animals and children. He'll tell you how he wants to improve the world in his own ways. Go to meditation classes and lectures on anything New Age and mysterious. Give him freedom to come and go, and find your emotional security elsewhere.

Pisces Girl and Pisces Guy

On the plus side: You'll be able to create your own unique reality to live in together and you'll be very happy there until the bubble bursts.

The negatives: Neither of you wants to look at how things really are, so you'll just end up on an emotional roller coaster you can't control.

Making the most of it: This is best when there are outside influences to keep things balanced. Keep a lot of friends around and even date other people once in a while. Volunteer together at an animal shelter or nursing home. Go out for runs around a lake and play on the swings. Make your responsibilities a priority and don't spend so much time together that everything else suffers.

Dumping

the

Guy

BREAKING UP WITH AN ARIES

Warning signals: Aries guys like to think the world revolves around them. Take that plus their live-in-the-moment attitude and you'll start seeing him disappear without considering your feelings. He'll also stop doing what he says he is going to do.

Dumping him: As much as you want to call him on things, the best way to tell him it's over is to say something like, "I think you are great but this is my problem." You don't have to believe that—you're just saving yourself a long, drawn-out ordeal. If you tell him how you really feel, he's just going to hear you blaming him for things and it'll get ugly fast.

How he'll really feel about it: Under all that bravado is a sensitive guy—he just doesn't like to show it. As you are laying out the bad news, he'll be hurt at first, but almost immediately his fiery, impulsive nature will take over and he'll get angry. He won't let you get the best of him. Whatever you say, he'll never think he did anything wrong to deserve this kind of treatment. The bottom line: He likes to be the one doing the breaking up.

BREAKING UP WITH A TAURUS

Warning signals: You'll know he's bothered by something when he quietly walks around brooding and doesn't reach out to help you as often. If you ask him what's wrong, he'll rarely tell you what's going on inside his head. It takes a lot for him to get mad, but once he is it's also hard for him to let it go.

Dumping him: Appeal to this guy's practical sensibilities and be honest. If you tell him that you went out with him because you thought he was special, but it's not right anymore, he'll understand. He probably won't ask you for an explanation. Be sure this is the right thing to do. Once you do this, don't expect him to take you back. He holds on to past hurts for a long time.

How he'll really feel about it: He'll definitely feel rejected but will try hard not to show it. Unless you really provoke him, you'll never see him explode, so you may even remain friends. He will have a hard time letting go, so expect some phone calls or e-mails from him about silly things.

BREAKING UP WITH A GEMINI

Warning signals: It's hard to keep a Gemini's attention. He's always flirty with everyone, so you might not know when it's innocent and when it's not. He'll sneak away to have some fun and tell you a little white lie just so you don't find out where he's really going. But he won't even call it a lie, more like an untruth.

Dumping him: He likes his chats direct and honest. You can tell him exactly what is on your mind and as long as you do it in a clever way, he'll listen to anything. Speak in full sentences, make a few sly jokes, and don't yell. He may give you a piece of his mind, too, but this breakup will come across more like a lively exchange than a final discussion.

How he'll really feel about it: This guy really rolls with the punches. You can say anything to him and he'll usually just accept it and move on. He has a great way with words, so if he's mad you'll know it, but the anger doesn't last that long and soon he's back to his detached self. He'll miss you for a day.

BREAKING UP WITH A CANCER

Warning signals: You know something is wrong in your relationship when your Cancer broods and refuses to give you an answer or a direct response. He gets easily hurt and doesn't forgive or forget. Instead he nurses his wounds in a childish way for all the world to see—oh, poor Cancer. If he doesn't want to snap out of this, he can hold on to it for a long time.

Dumping him: Go ahead and let your feelings out. Get as weepy and apologetic as you want and tell him exactly what's going on inside your head. If you do this right, he might actually feel sorry for you. If you criticize, blame, or get angry, watch out—the Crab is good at dishing it out, too. Be as gentle as you can. He's a sensitive guy and might feel badly about this long after you're gone.

How he'll really feel about it: He'll act as though you don't mean anything to him, but you'll be able to see deep in his eyes that he is upset. He doesn't take commitment lightly, so a relationship that goes off track can really get to him. If he didn't see it coming, it can take weeks to get over this. He can also get a tad vengeful. If you left something at his house after you broke up, you might get it back in pieces.

BREAKING UP WITH A LEO

Warning signals: At first he will put you on a pedestal and treat you like a queen. At some point, he'll realize that you aren't a statue and get the shock of his life. That's when he'll boss you around as if you are just a peasant. If this doesn't let up, fire him!

Dumping him: There is no good way to get rid of a Leo. Since he knows he is so fabulous, the only thing he is going to believe is that you have no choice but to leave him because he is too perfect, even for you. He'll take one millisecond to contemplate it and then will show his displeasure with you—and everyone else around.

How he'll really feel about it: He thinks he is so great that no matter how kind you are, he'll cause a scene. He'll make a big dramatic statement even if he doesn't care that much, just because he can. He might even dismiss you: "*You're* breaking up with *me*?" Actually, his lion-sized pride will take a big hit and he won't hesitate for a minute to blame you for it. He'll be mad for a long time.

BREAKING UP WITH A VIRGO

Warning signals: You'll know his feelings have changed when he is nitpicky about everything. This is his nature anyway, but when he is happy he finds things about you that he loves and hates. An unhappy Virgo will find fault with everything and nag you until you run out of patience—then there is a blowout. This is where he brings up everything on his tally sheet from day one. Ouch.

Dumping him: This is tough. He is a kind person with a calculating outer shell and a sensitive soul. You have to break through Mr. Critical before you can get to Mr. Nice Guy. On top of that, he looks down on emotion, so you can't tell him how you feel, or he won't listen. The key is to stay calm and appeal to his analytical side. Whatever you do, don't tell him what's wrong with him—you'll get a bigger list back in return.

How he'll really feel about it: On the one hand, he

will genuinely feel bad that things didn't work out between the two of you. He doesn't fall in love lightly, so if he let you into his life, you've got to be special. On the other hand, he has a cool detachment about him that thinks in facts and lists. This is the part of him that will justify not being hurt, because there were so many things wrong with you anyway.

BREAKING UP WITH A LIBRA

Warning signals: Libra guy is always searching in vain for the perfect love. The problem is that no matter how good it is, it might not live up to his ideal. Then it's just a matter of time before he loses interest. This is a subtle thing. He'll never come right out and tell you it's over, since that involves a realistic conversation. Look for his attention to fade away.

Dumping him: This will be very easy because the guy doesn't get mad. He avoids confrontation and feeling anything deeply. You can start off by giving him some space—he may naturally move on to someone who is more attentive. If that doesn't work, just tell him you want to see other people. The end. If you create a big scene, two things will happen: He'll be mortified at how garish you are, and he'll stop listening before his Libran scales fall off balance.

How he'll really feel about it: He is a pleasure-seeking guy, not one to harp on past hurts. He'll feel rejected for one minute, not because you meant so much but because he likes to have fans, and this means there is someone out there who doesn't admire him as much as he'd like. The only way he'd really get mad is if you said something that was unfair about him or the way things were. Then he'd definitely speak his mind, listing all the pros and cons and leaving you speechless.

BREAKING UP WITH A SCORPIO

Warning signals: Oh, you'll know when a relationship with a Scorpio is souring. He'll get untrusting, possessive, and jealous whether it is deserved or not. In his head he is thinking the worst, so he may even accuse you of things you didn't do. He is very good at uncovering secrets. If you're lying to him, he has no problem calling you on it.

Dumping him: There are two ways to deal with this temperamental guy. One is to walk on eggshells in an effort not to provoke him, and say good-bye as sweetly as you can. The second is to challenge him straight on and tell it like it is. If you do this, you better be sure of yourself, because this guy is a whirlwind of power and can make mincemeat out of the unprepared!

How he'll really feel about it: No matter how you start, within a nanosecond he'll bring the conversation to a boil. He takes your most innocent statements, twists them, and turns them back on you. He is emotional, intense, and he's also psychic, so he may actually figure things out and break up with you before you get a chance. That would definitely be easier on you—that is, unless you are another Scorpio! Also watch out that he doesn't sabotage your new relationship behind your back.

BREAKING UP WITH A SAGITTARIUS

Warning signals: It's not difficult to spot a Sag who has lost interest: He loses his attentive spark. That thing that made you feel so important to him goes, and he goes with it. He'll start showing up late or not at all. You can't ask him for an explanation—he won't have one, just that the time is up. He'll always want to remain friends if you don't leave him the wrong way.

Dumping him: You may never have to dump this one. When you're not having a good time anymore, just go off and do your own thing. That's what he would do. If you actually do have a conversation, keep it light; saying, "It's just not working for me" is plenty.

How he'll really feel about it: Chances are he won't be upset at all. If you went out for a long time, he'll be sad for a few days. But having the sorrow linger for a few weeks is highly unlikely. He'll definitely think about it. His philosophy will go something like this: "Too bad it didn't work out; oh well," and he'll waste no time moving on to the next person or at least look-ing with that constant restlessness that makes him who he is.

BREAKING UP WITH A CAPRICORN

Warning signals: Capricorns are tricky Goats. He can be hurt by something and never tell you; instead he holds it inside and keeps going as if nothing happened. When you look closely, you'll see an almost impercep-tible gloom mixed in with all that determination. The other thing he will do when hurt is pull his focus away from you and put it into his work, studies, and hob-bies.

Dumping him: He doesn't act out and rarely lets down his reserve, so you're free to break up however it feels natural to you. Just don't go out of your way to say hurtful things. If you push too many buttons, he'll explode.

How he'll really feel about it: Way under his cool exterior is a sensitive guy. It takes him a long time to fall in love, so if you managed to get that far into his heart, he will be hurt and stay that way for a long time. The hitch is that he will do whatever he can not to let you know that. On the other hand, if you never made it past his thick skin, he'll just shrug you off and go on to more important things.

BREAKING UP WITH AN AQUARIUS

Warning signals: He is a loyal guy who needs to know he always has his freedom. You'll know something is wrong when he starts to take advantage of that. He might come and go without explanation, but he can also be emotionally distant and seemingly unavailable. When he's with you but not with you, it's just a matter of time before one of you leaves.

Dumping him: He is usually very easygoing and takes an intellectual approach to his feelings, so you'll be through with it quickly by coolly saying what's on your mind. If you are the overemotional type and you provoke him, he'll respond the opposite way by trying to calm you down. If that doesn't work, he does have a temper—and he's not afraid to show it.

How he'll really feel about it: He's very busy with work, studies, hobbies, and outside interests. Chances are he never got that close to you to begin with. Whether you like it or not, he may not care all that much that you're gone. He can get attached to people when he feels they see the world the same way, and if you are one of them he will probably always care about you in his detached, impersonal way.

BREAKING UP WITH A PISCES

Warning signals: He loves to create the most romantic fairy tales to live in, but what happens when you want to get out? You'll know something is wrong when his deeply artistic fantasy gives way to harsh reality, and he'll do anything he can not to see things as they really are. He will seem indecisive and overemotional, and will run away at the first sign of problems. Don't chase after this elusive character—he's not worth it.

Dumping him: Be gentle. His feelings get hurt when you just look at him funny. Tell him he is a nice guy but be direct. He might want to hold on to you, so if you don't want to be friends, tell him that honestly. He'll get very sad and sulky right away and may try to make you feel guilty without actually saying a word.

How he'll really feel about it: No doubt he'll be very upset. Love is everything to him and rejection is the most severe penalty he can imagine. Oh, woe is me, breaking up with him plunges his emotions into turmoil—all his friends are bound to hear about it! Don't be fooled. He loves the emotional ride and he can bounce back like no other, but only when he is ready.

Getting Over the Guy

ARIES GIRL

You are independent, courageous, and energetic. Whether you broke up with your guy or he broke up with you, your insides tell you to get on with your life and your next adventure. You like to have a pal to follow you around, so you might get lonely for a short time, but you keep this inside and fill your day with activities. If you feel you've been treated unfairly, you get pissed off and have a temper tantrum. It can be hard for you not to let your sadness turn into hostility. You express everything, so it's easy for you to let things go.

You might try to figure out why it happened the way it did, but you'd come to a quick conclusion and tuck him away in the back of your mind. You need to know that it's okay to work it through, to try and understand the role you played in things instead of not wanting to think about it. That may be the best way to live and learn.

Words of wisdom: Keeping yourself busy is the fastest way to forget about him. It's also the best way for you to meet the next guy. You like to go to parties and be surrounded by friends. Your best philosophy: "I have courage to live my life through all experiences."

Best way to heal your heart: Let off some pent-up

steam by playing team sports. Go for a run or a hike in the park and wear yourself out. Find the biggest party and go there with your friends. If you run into him, don't say anything out of anger. Once something is said, you can't take it back.

TAURUS GIRL

Taurus girls don't make commitments easily and don't release them lightly—and that can be both good and bad. You don't flirt a lot, but once you get into a relationship you are very devoted. You'll do anything for your guy as long as you're appreciated. Because of this, you may find yourself getting the short end of the stick. Even with that, you don't get angry very easily. It's more likely that you'll walk away hurt and sulking than have an outburst.

Steady Taurus would rather deal with her smoldering feelings on her own than show him that she's mad. That's one reason why it takes longer for you to let it go—you process things very slowly. The other half of the equation is: You have so much built-in determination that you don't know what it's like to give up. You mull things over in a very methodical way, taking your time. Fixed and stubborn in nature, you have to come to your own conclusions, but it would help if you would open up and talk to your friends about these unresolved issues.

Words of wisdom: Learn to let go. Sometimes you hold on to things too tightly for your own good. Even if you were the one doing the breaking up, it probably took you a while to come to that resolution. Take this opportunity to increase your safety zone, find one of your more spontaneous friends, and do something crazy and fun. Let everyone know you're not brooding.

Best way to heal your heart: Go on an impromptu camping trip, have a barbecue on the beach, or take in a night at the theater. Work out your inner frustrations by listening to Bach or Mozart.

GEMINI GIRL

You never let yourself get into anything too deeply. This is a problem if your guy is trying to get to know you better, but an asset when you have just broken up with him. Since you probably weren't that emotionally connected to him to begin with, it becomes easier to let him go. In fact, you never felt like you had him to let him go in the first place. You have a very detached philosophy about love: You like to have fun with someone, experience something new, but once it gets boring or routine you lose interest and move on.

Even when you did love someone who broke it off, you can get emotional and angry that he is not there for you anymore, but as you catch yourself feeling something, another part of you is analyzing those feelings, doing more thinking than feeling. You're so quick to understand what happened that you begin to heal immediately. You can even be friends with him, and it won't bother you.

Words of wisdom: Instead of thinking so much about everything, take your time to process the relationship on a deeper level. Stop for a little while and take some quiet time to be alone and reflect. You won't be bored, and you may appreciate your experience better as a result. Either way, you're quick to get over it.

Best way to heal your heart: Change something for the better. Get a new haircut, have your nails done, or go shopping for a new hot outfit. Find a party to show it all off, be as chatty and flirty as you want and feel great.

CANCER GIRL

You more than most signs are affected by love. You search for an emotional commitment and will go far to get it. You aren't that easy to get to know, since most of your feelings are hidden behind a reserved outer shell. Once you find someone to attach to, you want to know them completely, spend every moment of the day with them, and share everything together.

You have great loves, but because you are so extreme, breaking up is really hard on you. Once you let someone into your life, you don't like to let them go. You need constant love and approval, and any hint of rejection weighs heavily on your mind. Spending a lot of time talking to your friends is your best medicine. Cry on their shoulders and slowly you'll begin to see the light at the end of the tunnel.

Words of wisdom: All relationships have two sides to them. Don't automatically feel like you are the only one getting your feelings hurt. Remember, he has his own unresolved issues—you aren't always the one to blame when things don't work out. Don't isolate yourself and harp on this over and over again. Sometimes it's good not to think about things too much. Force yourself to go out and have a good time.

Best way to heal your heart: See a funny movie with your friends, hang out afterward and let them cheer you up. Make sure you pick friends that are not only fun, but good listeners as well. Go out and help someone or something—visit an elderly neighbor, feed some birds, play with a dog.

LEO GIRL

Leos were born for romance. You thrive on love and are constantly looking for the perfect guy to complement you. You are outgoing enough to make the first move, but if you find that the guy isn't going to live up to your high standards, you'll quickly let him go and move on to another. The Lion usually ends up in the driver's seat; how much you dominate your relationship depends on what your guy will let you get away with.

You love being in love and think your guy is the best—that is, until he does something sneaky or deceitful. He will instantly move down a few notches and you'll dump him. On the other hand, if he dumps you, forget it. Your pride will be so hurt, not only because he got the better of you, but because you didn't see it coming. When that happens, you'll sulk for a time, but you won't allow that to get in your way for long. Immediately finding a new guy is the best medicine.

Words of wisdom: Don't get all upset because you can't control the situation and make it happen the way you want. Your pride can be your undoing. When you are breaking up, ask yourself: Are you doing this because you aren't getting along or is there another motivation at work here?

Best way to heal your heart: Plan a big party, get some friends to help you, go all out, buy chi-chi food and expensive entertainment. You'll have a great time being queen for a night and people will talk about it for a long time afterward.

VIRGO GIRL

Virgos don't take love lightly. You prefer to keep to yourself and hang out with your friends while you are waiting for the perfect guy, rather than go out and search for him. When you find a guy worth your time and attention, you slowly develop a deep bond that is not easily broken. You'll spend your days doing nice things for him, focusing your attention on the little details of love and life.

Since you took time getting into the relationship, you take your time getting out of it, too. You'll stick with him, but if you are not feeling appreciated you can get critical. If he doesn't respond, you'll cut your losses. You'll quickly fill your time with your serious-minded hobbies, but that doesn't mean you'll be over him. When you are hurt in love, you carry it with you under that calm exterior and just go on with your life. It might be a while until you allow yourself to love again, partly because you are hurt, but partly because you'd rather wait for another perfect guy.

Words of wisdom: Don't overanalyze the situation to see who was right and who was wrong. It could be that neither of you are at fault. Talk to your good friends about this. Sometimes another point of view will help you see things differently.

Best way to heal your heart: Grab your best friend, one who knows you well, and plan something you always wanted to do. Research foreign films and go see one. Find the perfect store to buy out-of-print books and go out of your way to get there.

LIBRA GIRL

Libras are built for partnerships. You look at romance as a necessity, another way for you to demonstrate your social graces. Affectionate, attentive, and adaptable, you make a guy feel like he is the most important thing since sliced bread. The downfall to loving you? Once you've charmed him, you won't stay unless he can keep your mind as well as your social schedule busy.

Since you'd do anything to avoid a conflict, you'll end every relationship with diplomacy—no matter how you truly feel about it. You look down on mud-slinging and emotional outbursts. The real test is finding a smooth way out. You may even try to remain friends with him after it's all over. You have no problem getting over someone who dumped you, either. You might get mad if he treated you unfairly, but you'll find a way to stay in balance no matter what. Plus, you know there are many more where he came from.

Words of wisdom: Don't take everything at face value; it's okay to look deeply into the dynamics of your relationship. If feelings come up, explore them. It might be better to see where they take you. Sometimes analyzing both sides of things stops you from experiencing all you can.

Best way to heal your heart: Go out and flirt. Charm the pants off of some new guys and add some admirers to your list. Buy something expensive—that always puts you in a good mood.

SCORPIO GIRL

Born under the most intense sign of the heavens, Scorpio girls love like no other. Even though you make the first move, you are wary of giving someone your whole heart. Once you're involved it can get intense pretty quickly; you like to know your guy to the bottom of his soul. You are kind, loyal, and mysterious on the one hand, possessive and jealous on the other. This makes for some unforgettable unions, but it also makes breaking up a bit of a mess.

You like to control the situations you are in—that plus your intense intuition, and you're likely the one doing the breaking up. Even if it's not your idea, you sense it's about to happen and take the lead. No matter how it goes down, count on some emotional eruptions and bad feelings for days or weeks to come, especially if you feel you got shafted. You get angry and resentful very quickly and have to take action in order to feel better.

Words of wisdom: If someone breaks up with you, don't automatically think the worst. Try to see the other side of things without making yourself crazy. Your first response might be to do something to hurt the guy back. Process everything before you do something you'll regret later.

Best way to heal your heart: Go to a meditation or yoga class. Practice martial arts to take the edge off. Find lectures on past lives or intuition to stay busy.

SAGITTARIUS GIRL

When it comes to getting over anything, Sag girls have it easy. You are such a free spirit that when something is over, you move on with not a care in the world. Since you are adventurous and outgoing, guys feel really comfortable talking with you. Once you snag them, though, it's a different story. If they hold on too tight, you start feeling claustrophobic and want to get out fast.

You can get attached to someone, but your nonchalant approach to love will never go away. Usually you'll do the dumping, so you may leave a few broken hearts lying around. Even if you are the one being dropped, you will never have resentment or hard feelings toward him. You can even remain friends and it won't bother you one bit. The only way you'd feel hurt is if he said some nasty things on his way out the door.

Words of wisdom: Don't run away at the first sign of problems. He just may not know something is bothering you. Give it a little time to work out before you quit. When you tell him how you feel, be honest, but make sure that you say it in the nicest way possible so you don't hurt his feelings.

Best way to heal your heart: Go on an adventure to a place you've never been before, explore a new park or a new part of town. Go to an amusement park and ride on the roller coaster a few times.

CAPRICORN GIRL

When it comes to love you are one tough cookie. You're very busy and don't have time for flirting and light chitchat. It takes a long time for you to commit to someone. You'll get to know him first and decide whether or not he is worth your time and attention. When you are in a relationship everything changes. You will stick by your guy through thick and thin.

Once you're in love, the person would have do to something really bad for you to break it off, but at least you can control how it goes down. If you are on the other end of things, it's a different story. Your pride doesn't take breakups easily. You might feel that he took advantage of your time and attention. You'll feel hurt and betrayed and that'll stay with you for a long time, but you won't let him see it.

Words of wisdom: You spend too much time being serious, especially after you've been hurt. Lighten up and try to go with the flow. Don't take everything personally and learn to let go of grudges. Hurt is not worth holding on to—you've better things to think about.

Best way to heal your heart: Find the most difficult crossword puzzle and finish it. Rent a funny movie, invite your best friends over to watch it, and let them cheer you up. Take up a new hobby: Pick something you've always wanted to try and tackle it like a nobody's business.

AQUARIUS GIRL

Aquarius girls like to do everything—friends, hobbies, even volunteer work. You like to be in love, but sometimes your free style gets in the way of deeper commitments. You want to have time for your friends and interests, so you tend to pick guys who give you space. If you do get involved with someone who is possessive or clingy, you quickly rebel. Being someone's girlfriend is not your biggest goal in life.

When you break up with someone, you are honest but are careful not to hurt their feelings. You are an idealist who likes to see the good in people, so you'll always find something nice to say. When someone ends it with you, it's easy to move on and remain friends. You can get annoyed if the breakup could've been done better, more fairly. You'll show your frustration but it is soon forgotten.

Words of wisdom: You are so busy thinking big you

should bring your focus onto your own life to understand your feelings better. Don't run at the first sign of emotion. You don't like clinginess, but learn to set boundaries instead of running for your life.

Best way to heal your heart: Go to a cool café and have a spirited discussion of the world's problems. Analyze why things happened and what you can do better next time. Call up your ex just to say hello, and tell him you'd like to be friends.

PISCES GIRL

You are so caring and compassionate that when you fall in love you get to know your guy to the depths of his soul. You smother him with kisses and love notes, making him feel like he is the most special guy in the whole world. Pisces are very changeable people—you have a way of becoming what he needs you to be. This can be good and bad, depending upon how much you change. Intuitive, you know exactly what to do to make him happy. The problem is that you are a little insecure and might question your hunches.

Since you fall in love so deeply and hang on so tight, you get really hurt when it unravels. You might even try to break up with him first just to save yourself some grief. This won't work because you feel everything so deeply. There is no greater rejection for a Pisces than to have your guy end it with you. You might feel like you have a broken heart for days or weeks. You'll quickly look for a strong and steady guy to take his place.

Words of wisdom: When you feel badly, don't isolate yourself—you could end up harping on negative thoughts over and over. There is no need to punish yourself after he is gone. Recognize how strong you are. Remember, guys are fun to be with, but you don't need him. Don't call him when it's over, and do what you can to avoid thinking about what he is doing now.

Best way to heal your heart: Invite a friend over to share a huge chocolate cake with you. Pour your heart out to her and cry all you want. Light a candle and talk to your angels. Ask them the best way to get over this guy, when you'll find the next one, and what you should do in the meantime.

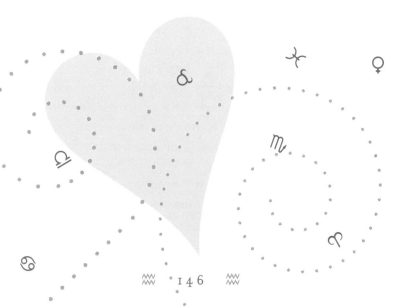

THANKS!

Thanks to everyone at Warner Books for their support and extraordinary efforts, especially my editor, Jackie Joiner, who has great vision and always has such super things to say about my writing! Stacey Ashton, thank you for ordering up another astrology book and knowing exactly what to do with it. Also, Lauren Lawson for the great publicity work. I'd also like to thank Les Pockell, Jean Griffin, and Jamie Raab. My appreciation goes out, once again, to my literary agent, Lisa Hagan, my parents, Harvey and Roberta Wolf, and my friend Maureen Jeffries for listening to me go on and on about astrology.

ABOUT THE AUTHOR

Stacey Wolf is a professional psychic and spiritual counselor in New York City. She has appeared on numerous TV and radio shows throughout the country, including *The View, The Late Show with David Letterman, The Roseanne Show,* and Joan Rivers's radio show. She is the author of *Secrets of the Signs* and *Get Psychic!* Stacey has been featured in *Mademoiselle* magazine and *The 100 Top Psychics in America.*